Presented To

On

By

LIFE ON PURPOSE™ DEVOTIONAL FOR TEENS

*Real Faith and Divine Insight
for Every Day*

LIFE ON PURPOSE™ DEVOTIONAL FOR TEENS

*Real Faith and Divine Insight
for Every Day*

By

Harrison House

Harrison House
Tulsa, OK

Unless otherwise indicated, all devotions written by Stephen Posey.

09 08 07 06 05   10 9 8 7 6 5 4 3 2 1

Life on Purpose Devotional for Teens:
Real Faith and Divine Insight for Every Day
ISBN 1-57794-682-0
Copyright © 2005 by Harrison House, Inc.

Published by Harrison House, Inc.
P.O. Box 35035
Tulsa, Oklahoma 74153

Contents

Introduction

How can your life be "on purpose"? How much of your life did you choose? It wasn't your choice to begin life when you did. Nor did you choose your family, your birth order, your race, or your gender. How, then, can your life be "on purpose"? Is there really a purpose for *your* life?

The answer is yes. God's purpose has been built into your very being. Psalm 139:16 says that "the days of your life were all prepared before you ever lived one" (MESSAGE). That means you were no accident. Your life is not a mistake. It's not a coincidence that you are who you are. God has an ordained purpose for your life from the beginning.

It's up to you to find and fulfill that purpose. *Life On Purpose for Teens* was written to give you perspective on God's ways. The more you know God, the more you will discover your purpose. As you read these real life applications of God's Word, may Christ be formed in you and may you truly begin to live *your* life on purpose.

Well Guarded

Guard your heart more than any treasure,
for it is the source of all life.

PROVERBS 4:23 NEB

"Down. Set. Hike!" Dad dropped back to pass in what had become a serious game of backyard football one Christmas break. I needed to make a big play. My younger brother, John, and I were playing for Christmastime bragging rights, and he was winning.

So as I took off running I looked back at my dad. To my surprise, the ball was already in the air. Dad had launched it! I turned it up a gear and ran as fast as I could, keeping my eyes on the ball the whole way.

Sure enough, the timing was perfect, but John was right there with me. As he jumped to try to knock the ball away, it sailed over his outstretched hands. I caught the ball, running at a full sprint!

I was so excited because I was about to score the game-winning touchdown. But just as I looked up from making the catch, *WHAM!* I ran right into a tree!

The collision knocked me flat on my back, and the ball fell out of my hands. I was stunned. I looked back at my brother to try and figure out what had just happened, only to see him rolling around on the ground in hysterical laughter. I had made all the right moves. I had done all the right things, but I left myself vulnerable to an unforeseen obstacle, and there I sat embarrassed and in pain.

You know, that's not unlike what can happen to us as Christians if we're not careful. We know our goal is a life of service to Christ. We keep our eyes on the prize. We go about our business doing good works, but if we don't guard our hearts, we are vulnerable to being wounded by the obstacles the enemy puts in our path.

Guarding your heart is not a matter of avoiding

LIVE ON PURPOSE TODAY

Think about the last incident in which your heart was wounded. Pray for any of the people who may have been involved in causing that hurt. Write down your plan to guard your heart if it happens again.

the pains of life. It's a matter of keeping your heart tender before God no matter what the circumstances. An unprotected heart becomes callused with each collision with pain. A callused heart becomes hard. A hard heart is too broken for relationship with God or with people. That's why the Bible tells you to guard your heart, "for it is the source of all life."

PRAYER

Heavenly Father, I pray that You give me a spirit of wisdom, so that I may discern the obstacles the enemy puts in my path. Enable me to guard my heart and keep it tender before You. In Jesus' name, amen.

Is This a Ten?

Vindicate me, O Lord, for I have walked in my integrity.
I have also trusted in the Lord; I shall not slip.

PSALM 26:1

It was the summer after my eighth grade year. Now that I was 14, my parents wanted me to bring in some cash of my own. I was still too young to get a "real" job, so I chose the honorable profession of lawn maintenance.

After going door to door, I landed a gig for a nice old man named Mr. Thomas. I was so excited. It was my first job! This guy was going to pay me ten bucks!

It took me almost two hours to do it right. Afterwards, I looked across that yard with great pride. It was a job well done.

I knocked on the door to tell Mr. Thomas that I was finished. "How much do I owe you?" he said. "Ten dollars, sir," I replied. Mr. Thomas pulled out his wallet. I had never seen so much cash in my life! He thumbed through $20's and $50's and loads of $100 bills.

But Mr. Thomas couldn't see very well in his old age. When he stopped thumbing he tugged on a $100 bill and asked, "Is this a ten?" I could not believe my ears.

All I had to do was say "yes" and I would have ten times as much money! No one would know. Besides, he had so much money he'd never miss it!

That split second seemed to last forever, but before I could think twice about it, I said, "No, sir." He found a real $10 bill and that was that.

They say integrity is about what you do when no one is looking. In my case, Mr. Thomas was looking, but he just couldn't see. No one knew the good decision I made that day...no one, except God.

LIVE ON PURPOSE TODAY

Take time to think through some of the situations in which you'll have to make tough choices when no one is looking (i.e. cheating on homework, looking at inappropriate Internet sites, etc.). Decide right now how you'll maintain your integrity in those situations.

But God never forgets the things we do in private to honor Him. God blessed me with great income that summer because I honored Him. In fact, since that one small decision on my very first job, I've had good income ever since.

Having integrity may not seem to pay off right away. It may even hurt at first. But as you trust God He will vindicate you. He never forgets when His children honor Him with integrity.

PRAYER

Heavenly Father, I thank You that You keep track of the little things I do for You. Strengthen me with might in my inner man today that I may walk in integrity and honor You. In Jesus' name, amen.

Of All People

A certain city was about to experience the wrath of God. For years, the people of this city had been enemies of God's people, Israel. It was a city of violent, hateful sinners. The city, Nineveh.

There was a man who strongly believed that Nineveh deserved the wrath of God. He knew that God was on his side, because he was an Israelite. This man was a prophet of God named Jonah.

If Nineveh were to fall, Jonah would rejoice. But God did something that Jonah could not comprehend. God told Jonah to take the message of repentance to Nineveh.

Jonah could not believe it! God was showing mercy to Nineveh?! They were, after all, enemies of Israel. Jonah was so much opposed to the idea that he did something really stupid. He boarded a ship with pagan sailors and fled Israel, attempting to run from God.

A horrific storm came, and the sailors feared for their lives. As the storm worsened, Jonah's heart softened. He knew that if he didn't do something, these men would die in that storm. So Jonah gave up his life to be thrown overboard, and immediately the storm ceased and the pagan sailors were saved.

But God saw Jonah's change of heart and provided a miracle. A great fish swallowed Jonah up. Jonah was buried in the belly of that fish for three days and nights until the fish spat him out onto the shore.

Finally, Jonah obeyed God and took the message of repentance to Nineveh. To Jonah's surprise, they listened! From the king on down to the commoners, the people repented and Nineveh was saved

LIVE ON PURPOSE TODAY

Consider the people outside the family of God in your sphere of influence. Write their names down. Before you go to sleep each night, pray for them to know the love of Christ.

from God's wrath. Jonah eventually saw that God's love was for all people, not just for his people, Israel.

As Christians today, it's easy to forget how much God loves sinners. As we surround ourselves with Christian friends (and rightly so), we must be careful not to become exclusive to those who don't yet believe. God went to great lengths to use Jonah to show mercy to the sinners of Nineveh. Jonah's story is a picture of how God would show mercy to the whole world through His Son, Jesus.

PRAYER

Father God, I thank You that You loved me so much that You sent Jesus to save me. Lord, I don't deserve Your love, but You give it freely. Help me to share that love with those who don't know You. In Jesus' name, amen.

All About Me

For I know the thoughts I think towards you,
says the Lord, thoughts of peace and not
of evil, to give you a future and a hope.

JEREMIAH 29:11

It was my first week at a new school. It was a big school. I didn't know anyone. No one knew me. So for the first few days I was able to go somewhat unnoticed.

That is, until my English teacher gave an assignment she was calling "All About Me." Every student was supposed to get up in front of the class and give a short autobiography, highlighting our hobbies and other interesting things about ourselves, using visual aids of some sort.

As I started putting together my presentation, I realized that outside of sports I didn't have any hobbies. So, I started going through my room to see if I could come up with anything else that might be interesting. I happened upon a stash of foreign coins my grandfather had given me, and I thought, *Aha! I have a coin collection! That's something interesting.*

Then came the day of my presentation. I got up and began to talk "All About Me." Everything was going great. My teacher seemed to perk up when I began to talk about my coin collection (which consisted of about seven coins).

"These two are Canadian coins," I said. "This one's from Mexico, here's one from Germany, and this one...." I paused for a second because I wasn't sure where this particular coin was from.

LIVE ON PURPOSE TODAY

Read 1 Samuel 30:1-19. See how David had unshakable confidence and self-esteem in the midst of terrible circumstances.

It had a picture of a guy wearing a turban. So, I made something up on the spot based on that picture. "This one is from India, and this last one...." My teacher interrupted. "Wait a minute; where did you say that last one was from?"

My heart started pounding as I said, "I think this one is from India." She tried to hold back her laughter as she said, "I don't think so. That's an Aladdin's Castle arcade token!" The whole class erupted with laughter. I was completely humiliated.

Why is it that so many of us tie our self-worth to what we do in life? I wasn't satisfied with the "me" I was presenting in my "All About Me" presentation, so I lied. A little white lie that had immediate consequences.

Christians, of all people, should have great self-esteem, not based on our performances or what we do in life, but based on who we are. We are children of God.

PRAYER

Father God, help me to see myself as You see me. I recognize
that You think good thoughts towards me and that,
with You, I have a great future. In Jesus' name, amen.

Vested Interest

*Let the Lord be magnified, who has pleasure
in the prosperity of his servant.*

PSALM 35:27

B y the end of his senior year in high school, a certain young man captured the attention of the whole world. His abilities on the basketball court had been seen on national television in front of millions of people.

In just a few short months, LeBron James was going to make NBA history, becoming the NBA's number one draft pick straight out of high school. Of course, that meant that in just a few short months LeBron was going to sign a contract with an NBA team for millions of dollars. Plus, with his instant celebrity status, he would be able to sign endorsement contracts for millions more.

However, for the time being, he had to wait on all of that...or so we thought. After his high school basketball season was over, the media noticed that LeBron was driving a Hummer H2, a very expensive vehicle.

LeBron was still living at home. His family's income was not sufficient to buy such an exorbitant gift. So, where did he get the money?

After the story broke about LeBron's new ride, we found out that it was his agent who fronted the $50,000 for the vehicle.

LIVE ON PURPOSE TODAY

Write down your financial goals for the next year (ex. college scholarships, a new car, a good job, etc.). Take these goals before God and ask Him to help you reach them.

The agent had a vested interest in LeBron. He wanted LeBron to look the part of an NBA star before he ever played a minute in the NBA. It worked. Not long after that, before he ever stepped foot on an NBA court, LeBron James signed a contract with *Nike* that would pay him millions of dollars over several years.

In a similar way, God has a vested interest in us, His children. Our lives are a message to the world around us. That message would not be effective if we all lived in a state of constant financial crisis. Therefore, God wants to see us prosper. He takes pleasure in it.

But the good news is, we don't have to drive $50,000 vehicles to make ourselves "look the part" of a person who is successful. No matter where we start in life, God can find small ways to prosper us so that the people in our world can see His goodness.

PRAYER

Father God, I pray that You enable me to present a strong
message of Your goodness to the world with my life.
I thank You that Your plan for me is to be blessed so
that I may be a blessing to others. In Jesus' name, amen.

Faith to Win

Every child of God can defeat the world, and our faith is what gives us this victory. No one can defeat the world without having faith in Jesus as the Son of God.

1 JOHN 5:4,5 CEV

It was the final event at the track and field competition, the 4 x 400 meter relay. I was going to be our team's anchor leg, which meant I was going to be the final person to run around the track and finish for our team. I was very nervous with this overwhelming task in front of me because we were going up against eight of the very best relay teams in the region, some of which had beaten us badly a couple of weeks prior. I entered the relay area with my team, unsure of my ability to help us finish strongly.

Right before it was my turn to get the baton, I heard God's voice inside say, *When I tell you to sprint, run harder than ever before and you'll fly like an eagle.* I was now even more nervous because I wasn't exactly quite sure when His voice was going to say, *Sprint,* and ask me to run harder than I had ever run before; and I wasn't sure if I was exactly up to this task. I got the baton in last place and took off running, and with about 275 meters left to run in the race I heard "sprint" inside, and I knew it was time to me to go. I had never run with

LIVE ON PURPOSE

Joshua recognized God's voice and had faith to obey it. As you continue to develop your own relationship with God, you'll begin to recognize His leading more and more often and have faith in what He says. He always has your victory in mind.

more might than I did once that word jolted through my being. I ended up passing seven runners and winning the relay race for our team, which was our first victory of the season. I know now that when God asks me to do something, I'll obey it because He always has our best in mind and our victory in hand.

PRAYER

Father, help me to recognize your voice—to be able to discern between my own ideas, the enemy, and Your voice. Help me to be diligent to study Your Word and to talk to You. Teach me to follow Your leading in every part of my life and to have faith in what You tell me, in Jesus' name.

Surf's Up

*And do not be conformed to this world, but be
transformed by the renewing of your mind....*

ROMANS 12:2

I t was a perfect day to learn to surf. The waves weren't
very high, the beaches weren't very crowded, and my
friends and I were very excited.

After a quick surf lesson on the beach, the guides
took us out to just the right spot and helped us catch a few
waves. Since I had never done this before, after about 30
minutes, I had completely run out of energy.

Exhausted, I decided to head back to shore. So I
located a landmark and began to paddle towards it. At first,
I wasn't paddling very hard. Then I noticed I wasn't getting
any closer to shore.

I started to paddle harder. To my surprise, that didn't
help. Not only was I not getting closer to shore, I was drift-
ing farther away from it!

At that point I realized that I was in the middle of a strong current. I immediately began to pray. I was beyond the point of physical exhaustion and would have had trouble swimming back without the resistance of the current, but I knew that I couldn't just let the current take me out to sea. Surely, that would have been disastrous.

As I prayed, God gave me wisdom and strength. I stopped trying to swim against the current. Instead, I swam parallel with the shore until I could get around the current. Finally, I reached the safety of the beach.

You may find yourself in a similar predicament in this life. Not that you'll literally get caught up in an ocean's current. No, the pressure that will try to pull you out to destruction is even harder to detect. The pressure you face is simply the pressure to conform to the world.

That pressure is like the current that tried to take me out to sea, relentless and

LIVE ON PURPOSE TODAY

Think ahead to situations in which you may be faced with pressure to conform your thinking or your actions to the world. Decide now, from a position of strength, how you will respond to those situations.

powerful. You may be able to resist for a while, but if you don't have a strategy, you won't keep up the fight for long.

The world's philosophies and desires are opposed to the ways of God, and, like the current that tried to take me out to sea, if you give in, you will be led to ultimate destruction.

So be faithful to renew your mind with the Word of God. It will give you power to overcome the pressures of this world.

PRAYER

Heavenly Father, I thank You for the power of Your Word to shape my thinking. I pray that You help me to continue to grow that I may not be conformed to this world. In Jesus' name, amen.

Hard Hat Area

{ *And take the helmet of salvation....* }

EPHESIANS 6:17

Being an accountant is not exactly what I would call a dangerous job. The words "white collar" come to mind. But in my uncle's case, I think a hard hat or a helmet should have been required.

One evening, my accountant uncle was supposed to meet my family for dinner. We weren't concerned when he didn't show up on time because it was in the middle of tax season.

But as soon as he walked through the front door, we became concerned. His face was flushed, and we noticed a big knot on his forehead.

He was hoping we didn't notice, but after we bombarded him with questions he explained. He had been diligently working on a very important client's taxes, and he was almost finished when, "all of a sudden I felt a sneeze coming on," he said. "I didn't want to sneeze on my work!" he continued.

Sitting down at the dinner table he showed us how, in that split second, he pushed back from his desk and sneezed a violent sneeze. The natural force of that sneeze caused him to throw his head forward and *BAM!* He slammed his head on the top of his desk with full force. He almost knocked himself out!

My dad thought that was the funniest thing he had ever heard. "He didn't want to sneeze on his work?" he repeated. "He didn't want to sneeze on his work!"

You know, the next time my uncle was at his desk and dropped a pen or something, I bet he was really careful to not hit his head on the desk. Who knows? Maybe he did wear a helmet!

You know, as Christians, we have access to protection in life that others don't have. But our warfare is not

LIVE ON PURPOSE TODAY

Study Ephesians 6:13-18 today. Write out the seven pieces of the armor of God. Hint: the seventh is spears—prayers (v. 18).

against physical forces. God has given us a spiritual "armor" to help protect the vulnerable areas of our lives.

We never have to worry about unexpected blows to the head when we take the helmet of salvation. Our thoughts can be protected from confusion and fear. And with the helmet of salvation, we're even protected from self-inflicted injuries, thoughts of self-pity and insecurity.

PRAYER

Father in heaven, today I thank You for equipping me with the helmet of salvation so that I can have victory in my thought life. In Jesus' name, amen.

A Big Job

Whatever your hand finds to do,
do it with all your might.

ECCLESIASTES 9:10

He was just a teenager, the youngest of eight brothers. Up until this time in his life, he had never done anything that most people would have considered significant. His family owned animals outside the city, so most of his day consisted of taking care of those animals. Basically, his job was the one nobody else wanted to do.

His older brothers, on the other hand, seemed to have it all together. They were much more developed physically. He was at times overlooked, overshadowed by his older brothers.

The three oldest brothers were not only more physically developed, but their jobs seemed to be so much more significant than his. While he was back home doing family chores, his three oldest brothers had joined the military and were off to war!

Surely seeing the success of his older brothers caused him to desire to do something more significant with his life. But he was just 15 years old. He was going to have to settle for doing the small tasks he had been given.

Even if he had dreams of significance, somehow he found a way to enjoy doing things that seemed insignificant. He began to take pride in caring for his father's livestock, protecting them from predators. In fact, he was known to have killed two of the most feared predators in that area.

There were times when his older brothers belittled what he did, but that never seemed to bother him. No one seemed to care about how hard he was working, but that didn't stop him from doing his very best.

LIVE ON PURPOSE TODAY

Write down the things in your life that you have been given to do right now (chores, job, school, etc.). Now write down three ways in which you can improve your effort in each of these areas.

Because he was faithful in the little things, God blessed him with great things. You may have heard of this young man. He soon became one of the most famous people in all of history. His name was David.

As you know, David was given an opportunity to do a big job: to kill Goliath, the giant. David greatly surpassed his brothers in significance in just one day!

All of us have a starting point in life. No one starts out at the top. There is a process involved in reaching our goals. Part of that process is learning to do our best wherever we are. Whatever your hand finds to do, do it with all your might!

PRAYER

Father, I commit to give You my very best effort in everything I put my hand to. Enable me to see the significance of my small tasks. In Jesus' name, amen.

A Well-Oiled Machine

{ *The fruit of the Spirit is…kindness.* }

GALATIANS 5:22

I knew not to expect to get a car on my 16th birthday. My dad let me know months ahead of time that, although my friends were getting new cars, that wasn't going to happen for me. We simply did not have the money for such a luxury.

But somehow, he found a way. It wasn't a new car. Far from it. It was 35 years old, in fact. But it was the coolest car our family ever had: a 1966 Ford Mustang with a 351 Windsor engine. I was thrilled to get it.

Soon I was driving all over southwest Georgia, gleaming with pride every time I had the chance to show my car off to someone new. I got to know that car like the back of my hand, and I did my very best to take good care of it.

One of the things I had to do on a regular basis was make sure it had plenty of oil. I wasn't really sure why it needed so much oil, but I did my best to keep up with it.

After a while, though, the newness of having this great car began to wear off. Slowly, I began to pay less and less attention to its needs. Yet, I was still depending on it to take me to the places I needed to go.

One swelteringly hot summer day my neglect came back to hurt me. It had been so long since I had checked the oil that there was scarcely a drop of it in the engine. My beautiful Mustang completely overheated and the engine was ruined. All because I did not understand the importance of oil.

I learned right away why oil is so important. It's a lubricant, meaning it helps the engine run smoothly and cuts down on natural friction. If only I had learned that a little sooner!

As you and I go through life,

LIVE ON PURPOSE TODAY

Think of one person close to you who you may be having conflict with. Show them one big act of kindness today!

our relationships are like the engine of a car. Sometimes there is natural friction. In fact, often the people we love most are the people who can cause the most friction.

Kindness is the oil, or the lubricant, of our relationships. Acts of kindness help smooth out possible friction. Kind words cool down heated arguments.

As we become more like Christ, His Spirit gives us the power to be kind in the midst of conflict. If we remember that, our relationships will run like a well-oiled machine.

PRAYER

Lord God, I pray for Your grace as I pursue kindness in all my relationships. Thank You for the strength to be kind in difficult circumstances. In Jesus' name, amen.

To Be a Son

Behold what manner of love the Father hath bestowed upon us, that we should be called the sons of God.

1 JOHN 3:1

They had not been married long, but Steve and Merrie knew right away what they wanted to do in life. Their aspirations were not driven by money, or fame, or success. Their simple desire was to make a difference in the lives of people.

So, they picked up their belongings, left family and friends behind, and took a job as house parents at a children's home.

House parents were couples that lived on-site with children who had been abused or abandoned by their parents. Steve and Merrie's assignment at this children's home was to take care of several young boys.

It didn't take long for the boys to grow attached to the young couple. Merrie would help them get ready for school. Steve would play football with them in the afternoons.

The feelings of connection were mutual. As Steve and Merrie saw what a difference they could make with these boys, their love for them grew stronger. They even tried to adopt one of the boys but were unsuccessful.

It was about this time that I was born at a nearby hospital. I was taken to this children's home to live with Steve and Merrie.

The rest of the boys welcomed me with open arms. It was as if I was instantly one of them. They loved getting to see the first few weeks and months of my life.

LIVE ON PURPOSE TODAY

Write down five benefits of being a child of God. Make a habit of thanking God for those things every time you experience them.

There was something different about me from the other boys, though. Sure, Steve and Merrie loved all of us a great deal. But when it came time for them to move on to their next stage of life, they couldn't take all of the boys with them, but they did take me.

What was different about me? Why did I get to go with this young couple that we all loved so much? Well, it's because Steve and Merrie are my parents. I was in that children's home not just as a child, but as a son.

The same is true for those of us who are followers of Christ. We are not just God's creation. We are His sons and daughters. He loves all of His creation, but our relationship with Him is special. We get all the rewards of son-ship.

PRAYER

God in heaven, I thank You that I am able to call You Father. Thank You for loving me enough to make me Your child. In Jesus' name, amen.

How To Become Great

{
A servant is not greater than his master; Nor is he
who sent greater than he who sent him. If you know
these things, blessed are you if you do them.

JOHN 13:16,17
}

The average citizen of New York City walks about four miles a day just going about their everyday business. That's a pretty good amount of walking. Most of us don't have to walk that much to get through our day-to-day lives.

Today, we take cars almost everywhere we go, but a couple of thousand years ago walking was pretty much the only option. Even though we don't do as much walking today, we have great shoes that keep our feet comfortable and somewhat dirt free. Back then shoes were not so comfortable and clean.

Can you imagine walking dirt and gravel roads with sandals? Your feet would be filthy! You would spend a better part of your evening shower scrubbing your feet. It wouldn't be the kind of thing you would ask anyone to do for you.

In Jesus' day it was the lowly task of servants to wash the feet of guests in a home. One night, Jesus and His disciples were eating supper together and there were no servants to wash the feet of the guests.

After supper, Jesus did something that surprised His disciples. He laid aside His outer garments and girded up His robe. Today we use the expression "rolled up his sleeves" to indicate that someone is about to do some hard work. Back then they "girded up their robes."

Jesus poured water into a basin and began to take on the subservient task of washing feet. He began to wash the filthy feet of these men that had most likely walked quite a bit that day.

Here was Jesus Christ Himself, a man whose popularity

LIVE ON PURPOSE TODAY

Find someone younger than you (sibling or friend). Think of how you can serve them in an unusual way (i.e. help with their chores or homework, drive them somewhere they'd like to go, etc.). Do that one thing today!

and fame had spread all around, a man who had done the greatest miracles the world had ever seen. Jesus, the Word of God in the flesh, on the floor with His hands in the mucky water, washing the feet of those who served Him.

Why did He do it? He did it so we could all see that in order to be great, we must serve. A heart of servitude is the key to going forward in the kingdom of God. Not that we ourselves should be served, but that we should serve others.

PRAYER

Lord Jesus, thank You for setting an example as to how we should live. Help me to find ways to serve others, so that they may see Your goodness. In Jesus' name, amen.

A New Season

{ To everything there is a season, A time for every purpose
under heaven...A time to weep, And a time to laugh; A
time to mourn, And a time to dance. }

ECCLESIASTES 3:1,4

New pastors, Jade and Christy. I liked them. They
were young and fun, but I'd had lots of pastors
over the years. Once you'd open up and let them
in, they'd move on, never to be heard of again. I'd like to be
friends with them. I'd like to be close to them, but if I'd
end up being just another face in their past, I'll pass.

Jade and Christy—they won me over. I opened up. I
let them in. We had a blast! We partied, learned about God,
ministered to others, went on missions trips, and prayed
until the compassion of Jesus rose up within us. Then the
news came. They were offered another position in another
state. But they had become such a big part of my life! When
I cried out to God, He took me to Ecclesiastes 3: to everything there is a season, a time for every purpose under

LIVE ON PURPOSE

When circumstances begin to change around you, you can find yourself unusually stressed and frustrated. That's when you know it's time to get into God's presence. Separate yourself from the world for a time until you get your "spiritual feet" again.

heaven. I had Jade and Christy for a season and now that season was over. I love them but now I know it's okay that they're leaving. I've been blessed, and it's time to open my heart for new relationships and the seasons God has for me.

PRAYER

Father God, when things are changing around me, I ask You to keep me stable. Help me to stay encouraged and to see the good in every circumstance. Speak to me through Your Word and let the peace of God rule in my heart, in Jesus' name.

Love Who?

You shall love your neighbor as yourself.

MARK 12:31

One evening I was tuned in to a popular sports television show. A certain man who had been in the headlines recently was being interviewed.

What he was saying might have been somewhat interesting, but I didn't hear a word of it. You see the man was wearing a t-shirt that had a message on the front, but the camera angle cut the message in half. For the duration of the interview I was trying to figure out what it said.

Eventually, the camera dipped down enough that the message could be seen. "I Love T.O." it read. When I finally saw it, I laughed.

You see the man wearing the t-shirt was one of the NFL's most flamboyant football players, Terrell Owens. Owens is known by most as "T.O."

In the midst of an interview in which he was being criticized about his behavior on the football field, T.O.'s not-so-subtle message to the world was, "I love myself."

Jesus was once asked, "Which commandment is the most important?" His answer was simple and powerful. "Love the Lord your God with all your heart, with all your soul, with all your mind, and with all your strength." And, "Love your neighbor as yourself."

Most people understand the "love your neighbor" part of the commandment, but what about the last part, "as yourself." Here, loving other people is directly tied with loving yourself. You may have never considered this before, but it's true. God wants you to love yourself!

God wants you to have a healthy perspective about who you are in Him. If you see yourself as He sees you, you'll be on the right track. The Psalms say you were "fearfully and wonderfully made."

LIVE ON PURPOSE TODAY

Pay attention to the words you say today. If you find that you're saying insulting things about yourself, correct that. If you find that you say overly prideful things, correct that.

Insecurity and self-hatred are not a part of the formula for fulfilling the most important commandment in the Bible. In fact, those things only cause you to spend more time thinking about yourself. It's hard to love other people if you don't love yourself.

So, love yourself as God loves you. When you do, you'll be able to love others and fulfill Christ's command.

PRAYER

Lord God, I thank You that You first loved me enough to send Jesus. I love You with all that I am. Help me to share that love with others. In Jesus' name, amen.

Santa's Giveaway

> *By this all will know that you are my disciples,*
> *if you have love one for another.*
>
> JOHN 13:35

Christmastime was always memorable in our home. Early on, my parents didn't have a whole lot of money, but they always seemed to find ways to make the season special.

I remember one Christmas Eve in particular, my little brother, John, and I were anxiously waiting for Christmas morning to come, when we heard an unexpected knock at the door.

Mom answered the door, and to our surprise, she called for *us*. We ran out to see who it could be. Sure enough, standing at our front door was Santa Claus.

I was old enough to know that this wasn't the real Santa Claus. It was someone dressed in a Santa costume.

John, on the other hand, was young enough to believe this guy was the real deal. But who was he?

I played along as John and I told Santa everything we wanted him to bring us for Christmas. Just as Santa was about to leave, John innocently whispered, "Santa Claus, my Dad has shoes just like that!"

Aha! At that point I knew. Santa Claus was, at least in this instance, my dad. He may have looked like Santa and talked like Santa, but his shoes were a dead giveaway. He was definitely our dad!

The more you and I follow Christ, the easier it is for people to recognize who we really are. We may walk and talk and look like mere men, but we're not. We are disciples of Christ. Jesus said that this will be clear to everyone by our love for one another.

LIVE ON PURPOSE TODAY

Write a special note of encouragement to a fellow Christian in your school.

Those of us who follow Christ have a certain sense of kinship with other Christ-followers. We want to see them succeed in life. We enjoy serving them. We have a sense of community that is peculiar to the rest of the world.

Our love for one another compels others to come to Christ. That's why it is important for us to take part in serving one another in a local church.

PRAYER

Father God, thank You for the love You have shed abroad in my heart. I purpose to let that love shine for You. In Jesus' name, amen.

The Shoeshine Boys

I say then; Walk in the Spirit, and you shall
not fulfill the lusts of the flesh.

GALATIANS 5:16

I recently visited Lima, Peru, with some friends. After we checked in to our hotel, my friends and I decided to patronize some of the local shops. We had no idea what we were about to encounter.

As soon as we hit the streets different people began asking us for money. One group of boys was the most persistent. None of them spoke English, but we could tell immediately that they wanted us to pay them to shine our shoes.

At first it was easy to refuse their offers because we didn't have much time. Then came Tony. Tony was a shoeshine boy, too, but there was something different about him. After we said "no" to Tony's friends they stopped asking. Not Tony.

Like a seasoned telemarketer, Tony didn't take "no" for an answer. "I shine," he'd say, piecing together what little bit of English he knew. "No, thank you," we'd say. But Tony was so adamant!

Finally, one of my friends decided to let Tony shine his shoes. After all, what could it hurt?

After Tony was finished, my friend gave him $5, a generous payment for 60 seconds of work. We were hoping this would satisfy the shoeshine boys so we could go on with our day. If only it were so.

Tony didn't seem to care how much he had been given. His only concern was to get more! Then the other boys began pleading with us after seeing Tony's success. We wanted to help all of them, but we realized they would never have been satisfied.

Our struggle with shoeshine boys is a lot like the struggle that

LIVE ON PURPOSE TODAY

Identify the fleshly desires you personally deal with the most (i.e. anger, lust, laziness, gluttony). Have a close, trusted friend keep you accountable in those areas for the next three weeks.

happens on the inside of people when faced with temptation. Because of our fallen nature, our flesh has an appetite for sin. It takes more than a strong will to overcome its desires.

Giving in to sin may pacify our flesh for the moment, but in the end it only awakens further desires. The desires of our flesh are insatiable.

The good news is Jesus didn't leave us powerless against the lusts of our flesh. In fact, He left His own Spirit to guide us and to enable us to overcome temptation.

PRAYER

Lord Jesus, thank You for the ability that You've given me to overcome the lusts of my flesh. I pray that You continue to lead me by Your Spirit today. In Your name I pray, amen.

One Expensive Meal

"I want it all, and I want it now!" could have been Esau's mantra. The firstborn son of one of the world's wealthiest men, this young man did, indeed, seem to have it all.

His future was determined. He would inherit the lion share of his father's wealth and have whatever he wanted whenever he wanted.

He was admired by most anyone who knew him. A talented sportsman, he, no doubt, garnered the attention of people everywhere he went. Life was good for Esau.

But one day his lust for the "here and now" cost him everything. Upon returning from an apparently unsuccessful hunting trip, he was exhausted and famished. His younger brother, Jacob, happened to be cooking stew at the time.

The aroma engaged Esau's senses, and it was too much for him to handle. He begged his brother to let him have the stew. "I am about to die!" he exaggerated.

Jacob shrewdly negotiated. He offered to give the stew to Esau in exchange for Esau's entire share of the inheritance. Because Esau was so used to giving in to the temptation of instant gratification, he agreed to the deal.

At first it may not have dawned on him how serious this mistake was. In fact, there were no immediate consequences for his decision. He was just happy that his stomach was satisfied.

But the day came when God honored Jacob instead of Esau. Jacob received the blessing of their father that was intended for Esau. On that day, Esau realized the weight of his decision, and although he cried and pleaded, it was too late.

Esau had auctioned off his future for one bowl of stew. What a terrible decision! No

LIVE ON PURPOSE TODAY

Exercise self-control over your flesh. Take five minutes to pray or read the Word before every meal today.

matter how good that stew tasted, no matter how satisfied he was after he ate it, it was not worth the cost.

That's how it is with instant gratification. It is never worth the price we pay in the end. No matter how good sin looks or feels or tastes, it's not worth auctioning off your future.

When you give in, there may not be instant consequences, but it will always come back to you and the cost will be more expensive than what you want to pay.

PRAYER

Father God, I thank You that my satisfaction is in You.
Give me wisdom today that I may not serve the
lusts of the here and now. In Jesus' name, amen.

A Higher Grade

Their trouble is that they are only comparing themselves with each other, and measuring themselves against their own little ideas.

2 CORINTHIANS 10:12 (LIVING LETTERS)

In a recent interview, Arnold Schwarzenegger, the foreign-born governor of California, was asked to "grade" himself for the work he had done thus far as governor. Apparently not being familiar with the typical grading system in the United States (A's, B's, C's, F's), his immediate response was "8."

I'll have to admit, when I saw that video clip on television, I laughed. But the more I thought about the situation, the more appropriate I thought his answer was. Most people in California agreed that Governor Schwarzenegger was doing a pretty good job at that time, but Arnold's answer revealed to us that his standard of measure in grading himself in life is different than most.

In 1962, as an Austrian teenager, Arnold Schwarzenegger decided exactly what he wanted to do with his life. He didn't see himself going to law school or becoming a doctor. His goals were unique. In fact, I'm sure many people around Arnold doubted he would ever go very far with his peculiar aspirations.

But Arnold was not discouraged. He trained and trained until he was at his best. At the age of 18, Arnold won his first body building competition.

By thirty, Arnold had far surpassed the expectations of his family and friends. After investing his money wisely, he was already a millionaire. Most would have stopped there. Not Arnold. He continued to compete at his best, winning Mr. Universe five times and Mr. Olympia seven times.

LIVE ON PURPOSE TODAY

Revisit your goals and dreams. Write them down and take a step each day towards reaching them.

In 1983, Arnold became a citizen of the United States and embarked on even more ambitious dreams. For the next two decades he landed starring roles in several hit movies.

Those who doubted him early on in life were a distant memory, and Arnold had become a success. He succeeded, not because he surpassed the expectations of others, but because the expectations of others were never a part of the equation.

As followers of Christ, you and I have been given a different standard by which we should measure our lives. Common people take a look around them and use their peers or their own families as a personal standard of measure.

Christ came to show us how to live. His life is our standard of measure. If our life's pursuit is to be like Christ, we will rise above the fray and truly be successful.

PRAYER

Lord Jesus, I thank You that You not only showed me how I should live, but You empowered me by Your Holy Spirit to be able to do so. In Jesus' name, amen.

Transformed

{
*And do not be conformed to this world, but be
transformed by the renewing of your mind, that
you may prove what is that good and acceptable
and perfect will of God.*

ROMANS 12:2
}

I was always a social kid and had lots of friends. During
my sophomore year of high school, my dad's job
transferred us to another city. I had to start over at the
beginning of my junior year in a new school where I knew
no one. It was a shock to me that I was not accepted right
away. I felt terribly lonely and rejected. There was nothing
my parents or I could do to change the situation. In my
desperation, I turned to God. I cried out to Him for help
and spent time with Him every day seeking His love and
His direction for my life. The most amazing thing started to
happen. All those feelings of needing to be accepted by
others began to disappear. Instead, my confidence began to
grow in Christ. I became rooted and grounded in His love,
and the love of others became secondary. I did eventually

make friends, but I will be forever thankful to the Lord that I was able to find Him.

LIVE ON PURPOSE

If you have been struggling with your self-worth, take some time to find out who you are in Christ. Look up all the Scriptures in the New Testament epistles that say "in Him," "in Whom," or "in Christ."

PRAYER

Lord, I do not want to be conformed to this world, but I want to be transformed by the renewing of my mind. Help me to understand who I am in Christ Jesus. Help me to break away from negative influences of the world that damage my self-worth. Ground me in Your love and faithfulness, in Jesus' name.

Are You Ready?

And everyone who has this hope in him purifies himself, just as he is pure.

1 JOHN 3:3

"Thanks for letting me use your apartment," I said as my friend Ryan walked out the front door of his second-floor living quarters. Ryan often let me use his apartment so I could study during my second year of college.

That night, however, I was feeling a bit mischievous. When Ryan closed the front door I jumped up and peeped out the window to see him round the corner. When it was clear, I ran outside and darted around the other end of the building. I had a simple prank in mind.

I knew it would take him a while to find his car and get situated. My plan was to take off running down the street and get as far away from the apartment as I could.

When he finally drove down the street, I wanted him to see me walking back towards the apartment and wonder how in the world I got there. What actually happened was far better than what I had planned.

What I didn't realize was that as soon as I left the apartment, Ryan came back! He had apparently left something behind. As he came back in the front door, he called out to tell me something, but of course I didn't respond. I was a half-mile down the street!

In his mind, there was no way I could have left the apartment in that short a period of time, so he started looking to see if I was hiding. The more he looked and didn't find me, the more freaked out he became.

LIVE ON PURPOSE TODAY

Take account of your life today. If Christ were to return, would you be ready? If not, make the change.

The thought that was in the back of his mind became more and more prevalent: "Did I miss the Rapture?" He called his aunt and uncle, who he knew were both right with God. For whatever reason, they weren't home! He really started to believe he was left behind.

Finally, I showed up again at the front door. Boy, was he relieved. Later he admitted that it was a good scare. It caused him to wonder, *If Jesus really did come back, would I be ready?*

Knowing that we could be face to face with Jesus at any moment causes us to want to live right. As Christ-followers, you and I should *plan* our lives as if Jesus is not coming back in our lifetime, but *live* our lives as if He's coming back today!

PRAYER

Lord God, if there is any hindrance in my life to a pure relationship with You, I ask for Your forgiveness and I repent. In Jesus' name, amen.

Who Needs Enemies?

Do you not know that friendship with the world is enmity with God? Whoever therefore wants to be a friend of the world makes himself an enemy of God.

JAMES 4:4

W hen I was a boy, there was a 17-year-old guy from our church whom I looked up to. We'll call him "Charlie." He seemed to be a pretty cool guy. But one night, he not only lost my respect, but he lost his family and his freedom.

It was about 1:30 A.M. The family was fast asleep when Charlie heard a "tap, tap, tap" on his bedroom window. He pulled back the curtains to see who it was. It was a friend from high school.

So Charlie grabbed his coat and crawled out the window. As he and his friend ran down the street, they met up with several more friends, one of which had a car.

Charlie didn't know what they were going to do that night. He was just looking for fun.

After driving around for about an hour, they stopped the car in the back alley of a furniture store. "Charlie, you're driving!" Everyone but Charlie jumped out of the car and headed towards the building.

Charlie's heart began pounding. His palms began to sweat. He realized that something wasn't right. But he couldn't just leave them there! They were his friends.

All of the sudden, the guys came running towards the car. One of them had a television in his hands. Another had a VCR. Charlie could hear the security alarm blaring as they piled into the back-seat. "Go, Go, Go!" they screamed.

LIVE ON PURPOSE TODAY

What influence do your friends have on you? If they are pulling you away from God, choose new friends.

By now, Charlie was scared out of his wits. The tires squealed as they sped out of the alley and onto the streets. Finally they reached the neighborhood where Charlie lived.

He thought the nightmare was over, but it had only just begun. They were surrounded by police cars in an instant. They were caught!

Charlie hadn't stolen anything, but that didn't matter to the police. Charlie was guilty. He was an accomplice to a theft and was on his way to jail.

Charlie's poor decision-making happened long before he snuck out of the house that night. He would go to juvenile prison for theft, but Charlie was most guilty of choosing the wrong friends.

That next day, my father told me what happened to Charlie. He loved me enough to teach me the importance of choosing the right friends.

PRAYER

Father God, I pray that You help me find good friends who love You as much as I do. I thank You that You are a friend who sticks closer than a brother. In Jesus' name, amen.

Speck-tacle

And why do you look at the speck in your brother's eye,

but do not consider the plank in your own eye?

MATTHEW 7:3

Justice. There is something inside all of us that naturally cries out for it. When we see injustice in our world, we want to do whatever we can to make it right. Especially when the injustice seems to have occurred against those we love.

Sometimes, however, our sense of justice can be distorted. There are times when we cry for swift justice against those who have wronged us, while expecting unconditional mercy for our own behavior.

The following conversation occurred between my younger brother, John, and my mother several years ago. Keep in mind that John was only about three years old.

"Momma!" John cried. "What's wrong, son?" said Mom, with concern. "Stephen hit me on my back!" John explained.

"Aw, I'm sorry, son," Mom said. John continued to cry. "It really hurt," he said. Mom sensed that John was looking for sympathy, so, in her motherly wisdom, she investigated. "Okay, what were you doing when Stephen hit you on your back?"

John paused, thinking back to what he was doing the exact moment in which I hit him on his back. "Screamin'," he said.

Trying to hold back her laughter, Mom explained. "No, I mean what were you doing before he hit you on your back?" Finally, the truth came out. "I was drinkin' his coke," he said.

Many of us fail to consider all the facts when we accept the label of "victim" in certain situations in life. It is not

LIVE ON PURPOSE TODAY

What areas do you tend to be the most critical of people? Consider how you stack up in those areas in light of the Word.

uncommon for us to overlook our own faults when we point out the failures of others.

Even in telling that story, I've made myself out to be somewhat innocent, omitting the fact that there were several other times in which I antagonized John without him provoking me to do so.

Jesus warns us to be careful in passing judgment on people. To be a righteous judge of people means we must consider all of the facts in light of God's Word, including facts about ourselves.

That's why Christ warns us not to pass haughty judgments on people. You and I are righteous before God, but that righteousness is not because we have never sinned. It's only because of God's grace.

PRAYER

Lord Jesus, I thank You for the righteousness You've given me before God. Help me not to pass prideful judgments upon people. In Jesus' name, amen.

Bubba

{ *When he, the Spirit of truth, has come,*
he will guide you into all truth.... }

JOHN 16:13

Bubba didn't mean to be funny, but he was. That was partly due to the fact that he was kind of funny looking. He had one lazy eye and a slow, wide-mouth yawn. He wasn't the best looking or the smartest character around, but he definitely made us laugh.

That's how I remember Bubba—our cat. All cats have their peculiarities, but Bubba seemed to be more peculiar than most. He always seemed to be falling off tables and running into things, but somehow he outlived all of his brothers and sisters.

As I recall, one of my siblings went outside to feed Bubba one morning but couldn't find him. As we all began to search for him, we heard a series of desperate "meows." We realized the sounds were coming from somewhere up above us.

We looked up at a giant pine tree that had no branches until about 50 feet up in the air. Sure enough, there was Bubba, 50 feet high, sitting on a branch.

Bubba had obviously been there all night long, not knowing how to get down. The night before, a pack of stray dogs had apparently come through and chased Bubba up the tree. Bubba was so scared that he scaled 50 feet straight up!

My brother and I moved the trampoline under the tree and took every ball we could find to try to knock Bubba off the branch onto the trampoline. Finally, after several tries, we were successful.

LIVE ON PURPOSE TODAY

**Read Acts 16:6-10.
See how the Holy Spirit
led Paul and his ministry
team from city to city.**

The ball hit Bubba with just enough force to knock him out of the tree. As he fell, Bubba was discombobulated, flailing about in the air. Eventually he caught his balance and safely landed *on his feet* on our trampoline.

Cats have an amazing sense of balance that way. It's almost as if they have an internal compass that enables them to know which way is which.

As a believer, you have such a tool on the inside of you. When Jesus left us His Spirit, He said the Spirit would guide you into all truth.

Therefore, you have an internal compass that allows you to know which direction you should go in the most confusing situations. When you feel discombobulated in life, the Holy Spirit will help you land on your feet.

PRAYER

Lord Jesus, I thank You for sending Your Spirit to be my guide in life. I submit to Your guidance today.

Do as Dunant

{ *Execute true justice, show mercy and compassion everyone to his brother.* }

ZECHARIAH 7:9

Jean Henri Dunant was just a young man, a Swiss banker visiting Italy on a trip through Europe. He had nothing to gain by getting involved in the affairs of others. But what he saw that fateful morning changed his life forever.

As he walked out onto the field at Solferino, he was horrified. He saw 40,000 men dead or wounded from battle. And no one was there to care for the wounded! No one was there to care for the corpses of these men who had given their lives for their countries.

These images would be indelibly marked in his memory forever. He could have found a way to forget about what he saw. He could have just continued his tour of Europe, hoping someone else would do something.

But Dunant was full of compassion. He could not bear to walk by passively and do nothing. So he wrote down everything he saw in a book called *Recollections of Solferino.*

At the end of his book, Dunant pleaded with all who read it, "Would it not be possible to found and organize in all civilized countries, permanent societies of volunteers who in time of war would give help to the wounded without regard for their nationality?"

Dunant published his book, and within one year, he had inspired the world to make a change. Delegates from 16 nations met with Dunant to talk about his idea in the first Geneva Convention.

LIVE ON PURPOSE TODAY

Find a way to help someone in need today! (Volunteer time, give money to your church or a compassionate organization, etc.)

Out of that meeting, an organization was formed that would recruit volunteers from several countries to work together in times of war and crisis to provide aid. That organization still exists today, some 140 years later. The organization is called The Red Cross.

From that time on, many countries joined together in agreement to treat civilians, prisoners, and battle-wounded persons in a humane manner. Those treaties also still exist today.

Dunant was just a young businessman in a foreign country. He could have looked the other way, but he didn't. Dunant's decision to do what was in his power effectively changed the world forever.

You and I are called to have compassion on individuals in our world. Living a life of compassion towards others, showing mercy to those in need, is a life not consumed with "self." Such a life can make a difference. Such a life can, in fact, change the world.

PRAYER

Father God, I thank You for the compassion that You have towards the helpless. I pray that You would enable me to live a life of compassion towards others. In Jesus' name, amen.

Disappointments

Direct my footsteps according to your word;
let no sin rule over me.

PSALM 119:133 NIV

I didn't make the cheerleading squad. Nursing my sorrows, self-pity, and the cumbersome chip on my shoulder in a jumbo bag of potato chips, I mentally ran down my list of twenty-one questions: "Why, God, why? Why did this have to happen to me? Were my cheers not good enough, loud enough, exuberant enough?" I renounced sins I hadn't even committed and even rebuked the devil for stealing and devouring my fifteen minutes of fame. Suddenly, my father's story arrested my self-destructive train of thought.

"An ant depends on its antennae to map out its surroundings," he said. "When an ant senses that a human finger or foot is nearby, it scurries away and changes direction. God often pushes us toward our destiny even though we cannot see it. Somewhere between His finger and our frenzy, we'll walk right into the place where He wants us to be."

This setback was merely God's divine setup for a comeback. During high school, one of the school's news anchors moved to another state, leaving a vacancy...and an opportunity. I felt the Holy Spirit tell me to try out for the position. I loved to read and write, but I had my reservations. I did not want another rejection. Yet, I surrendered to the Holy Spirit and tried out. Four years and hundreds of stories, weather reports, and interviews later, I found my niche in broadcast journalism.

LIVE ON PURPOSE

When you experience disappointment, get in prayer about it right away. Allow God to turn those situations for good in your life—to help push you toward your destiny. He has a specific plan for you, and He wants you to discover exactly what that is.

PRAYER

Father, I want You to order my steps according to Your Word and Your plan for my life. Give me wisdom to make good decisions. Help me to be strong even in the face of disappointments. I know You have a plan for me that will satisfy the desires of my heart, in Jesus' name.

How To Get Your Dream Job

Delight yourself also in the Lord and he shall give you the desires of your heart. Commit your way to the Lord, trust also in him, and he shall bring it to pass.

PSALM 37:4,5

When he closed his eyes he could still see it. The pictures were as vivid as the first time he saw them in his dreams. Someday he would be an honored ruler. But that day seemed further away than ever for Joseph.

Imprisoned for a crime he did not commit, in a land far removed from the people he knew and loved, there sat Joseph, alone. What happened to the dreams he had dreamed as a 17-year-old young man?

Three times he had found great favor in the eyes of those whom he served. Three times he had been betrayed.

At this point, Joseph's dreams seemed like a cruel joke in the face of reality.

He had been his father's favored son, sold to slavery by his brothers. Yet as a slave, he found favor with his master. There, Joseph was put in charge of all of the other servants, only to be falsely accused by the master's wife.

His master had no choice but to throw him in the king's dungeon. Somehow Joseph found favor again, this time with the prison warden. There he served prisoners of the king. Two such prisoners had important dreams in the night. God gave Joseph the interpretation of those dreams and Joseph told them. One of the men was freed, yet he forgot Joseph's kindness.

So there, helplessly, he remained in prison. He had been given every opportunity to give up, yet he kept on serving. He had been given every opportunity to develop bitter hatred towards

LIVE ON PURPOSE TODAY

Encourage your dreams.
Read Genesis 37, 39-45.

those who had betrayed him, yet he kept a good attitude. He had good reason to be angry with God, yet his heart remained tender before Him.

This was Joseph's secret. He did not let his circumstances dictate his fate. Therefore, God prospered Joseph at every stage of his life.

After 13 years of being victimized, betrayed, wrongfully accused, and imprisoned, Joseph was promoted to ruler of all Egypt, second only to Pharaoh, the king.

Joseph never let go of the dreams God had given him as a young man, and they came to pass. His attitude helped him achieve the job of his dreams.

God has a plan and purpose for your life. He is the One who designed you and placed dreams in your heart. If you keep Him first and commit your way to Him as Joseph did, you too will achieve your dreams.

PRAYER

Father, I put my trust in You. What is impossible with man is possible with You. In Jesus' name, amen.

Your Acquittal

Put me in remembrance; Let us contend together;
State your case, that you may be acquitted.

ISAIAH 43:26

"These people are stiff-necked!" God was not happy with the Israelites. After He had brought them out of slavery and performed many miracles to protect and provide for them, they quickly forgot Him.

After the people attributed all of God's glory to an idol they themselves had created, God was ready to remove His favor from them, allowing them to be killed. He was deeply grieved by their pride.

God offered Moses a deal that most people would have jumped at. It wasn't that God was trying to tempt Moses, because God can neither tempt nor be tempted. God was testing Moses' heart to see if he was a worthy leader.

The deal was that God would remove His favor from the Israelites and grant His blessing solely to Moses and his progeny forever. Moses passed the test.

Moses could have considered the possibilities of life without the headaches of leading these people, but he didn't. Instead, Moses had compassion on them and identified with them. He immediately began to plead their case before God.

LIVE ON PURPOSE TODAY

Use Scripture to make a case for your area of need, as if you're an attorney. Plead that case before God.

"Turn from Your fierce wrath," he pleaded. "Remember Abraham, Isaac, and Jacob, Your servants, to whom You swore by Your own self…" he continued.

Moses was innocent, yet he identified himself with these sinful people in order to save them. He reminded God of His own Word. God was pleased with Moses and relented from allowing the Israelites to be harmed.

This is one of the great pictures of God's heart towards sinners. God knew that Moses would plead the case of the people. He wanted to see Moses intercede on their behalf.

Jesus shed His own innocent blood so that you and I could be acquitted before God. Our sins are forgiven because Jesus, the righteous, identified with us, the unrighteous. His sacrifice freed us from sin and all of its effects.

Therefore, when you and I face problems in our lives, we must learn to plead our case before God. Just as Moses did, God wants us to remind Him of His Word.

PRAYER

Heavenly Father, I thank You for Your Word. I believe that Jesus' blood has covered my sins. In Jesus' name, amen.

Inside Hindenburg

It was the first commercial passenger air service across the Atlantic Ocean. Understandably, after proving to be successful, the Zeppelin LZ 129 Hindenburg became quite popular.

In 1936, Hindenburg was the world's largest aircraft. It was almost as long as a regulation football field and could travel up to speeds of 78 miles per hour.

After a successful first season of flights across the Atlantic, the owners of Hindenburg increased its seating capacity. The first flight of the second season packed in 97 people.

That first flight went according to plans across the ocean, but as Hindenburg approached its mooring mast in New Jersey, disaster struck. Somehow, the mix of the materials that cloaked Hindenburg and the hydrogen inside it ignited.

The zeppelin instantly exploded, and within a period of minutes the entire aircraft was destroyed. Thirty-five people died. This catastrophe brought an end to passenger service in such aircrafts.

No one knows what caused the hydrogen to explode inside Hindenburg that day, but it is known that the creators of Hindenburg did not intend for it to be filled with hydrogen at all.

Although hydrogen was an okay substitute up to that point, the creators' original intent was that Hindenburg be filled with helium. Unfortunately, if Hindenburg had been filled with helium instead of hydrogen, the tragic explosion would not have happened.

There are many things you and I can fill our lives with. The variety of choices we have today are

LIVE ON PURPOSE TODAY

Set aside some extra time to pray in the Spirit and worship God today.

exponentially more abundant than that of the generations that have gone before us.

We literally have thousands of things we could choose to do in a day that would provide some kind of stimulus for us: sports, television, music, movies, reading, chatting on line, talking on the phone, going out to eat, playing video games, computer games, etc. The list could go on and on.

The Word of God implores you and I to be watchful of what we fill ourselves with. You can choose to constantly fill your life with any of the things this world has to offer, but those things are only substitutes.

Your Creator designed you to be filled with something much better. The Bible tells us not to be drunk with wine (worldly stimulus), but be filled with the Holy Spirit.

God wants you to enjoy the abundance of choices you have in life, but ultimately if you seek those things first, they will be a poor substitute. Only the Spirit of God can truly fulfill you.

PRAYER

Dear Jesus, I thank You that when You ascended into heaven, You left us Your Spirit. I ask You to fill me with Your Spirit today. In Jesus' name, amen.

A Fruitful Invention

J ames loved competition. As a young man in Canada, he found that he was gifted in both lacrosse and rugby, two of the world's roughest team sports. Soon James became known as one of Canada's best athletes.

After attending college in Montreal, where he studied for the ministry, James moved south to the United States to become a physical education instructor. He found a job in Massachusetts at a school for Christian workers.

In the cold winter of 1891, James's boss gave him an assignment. He was to come up with a team game that the students could play indoors during the winter. So James went to work on a new game.

He started with what he had. He looked through the different kinds of balls he could use and decided he needed something large enough people could easily catch. So he grabbed a soccer ball.

As he looked at the room in which he was to play his game, he remembered the balcony. The railing from the balcony hung about 10 feet from the floor. Then came inspiration.

He asked the school superintendent for a couple of boxes that he could hang from the balcony railing. Instead, James was given a couple of wooden peach baskets. The students could attempt to throw the soccer ball in the basket! It worked.

James Naismith had no idea how popular his game would become. He had invented the game of basketball. Over the next 100 years, millions of people would enjoy his invention, playing basketball in schools or backyards, or watching in arenas and on television.

Ideas are God's currency. When you and I ask Him for things,

LIVE ON PURPOSE TODAY

Consider your biggest needs today. Meditate on Philippians 4:19. God will show you the solution.

He gives them to us in the form of thoughts and ideas. The more we meditate on God's Word, the more open we are to those thoughts and ideas.

The verse above tells us that wisdom dwells with prudence. Prudence is simply "a careful management of one's resources." James Naismith started with the things he had. That's what God wants us to do with our resources.

If we will start with what we have and meditate on the Word of God, He will give us creative ideas and knowledge of witty inventions that will help prosper us in everything we do.

PRAYER

*Father God, Your Word says that You freely give
wisdom to those who ask for it. I pray that You
fill me with Your wisdom and the knowledge
of witty inventions. In Jesus' name, amen.*

Prayer Power

As a preacher's kid, I had been with my dad in several circumstances in which people were desperate for God's help. Whether I intended to or not, I picked up little things from him when he prayed. He always prayed with confidence, and his prayers were full of the Word of God.

When I was fifteen, I found myself in a situation in which I was going to have to draw from those experiences whether I wanted to or not. One cool, rainy evening in early spring, I was invited to play basketball in an old gymnasium downtown.

As soon as our feet hit the old tile floor, we noticed that somehow condensation had risen up from under the foundation. There weren't puddles of water, but it was just wet enough that the floor was slippery.

We decided to play basketball anyway. Just as we expected, the condensation added an extra element of fun as we slid across the court like hockey players on the ice.

We were having a blast, until something bad happened. One guy, named Mike, tried to see how far he could slide and stay on his feet, but he lost his balance. His feet slipped right out from under him. Airborne for what seemed like a minute, he fell backwards and landed on his head.

We all heard the chilling thud of his head against the old tile floor and looked to see if he was okay. Mike jumped right up and started laughing, but after he took a couple of steps he fell back to the floor. All of a sudden Mike started violently convulsing.

The blow to his head had caused him to go into a seizure. Mike's brother tried to wake him from his condition. Nothing happened. After a few seconds, Mike's face turned blue. Someone wisely suggested, "He swallowed his tongue!"

LIVE ON PURPOSE TODAY

Learning to pray with confidence in the Word is a matter of practice. Find a place to be alone and start today.

A friend and I stepped to the side and immediately began to pray for Mike. Using what I had learned, I prayed with confidence in God's Word that God would help Mike in those crucial moments.

Finally, they were able to pull Mike's tongue from his throat and he started breathing again. The paramedics arrived and rushed him to the nearest hospital.

Mike could have suffered permanent brain damage or could have died from his accident that night, but he didn't. God saved him from destruction and answered the prayers of two righteous teenage boys.

PRAYER

Father God, I thank You that I can have confidence in You when I pray according to Your will. In Jesus' name, amen.

No Fear, Part 1

Let no one despise your youth, but be an
example to the believers in word, in conduct,
in love, in spirit, in faith, in purity.

1 TIMOTHY 4:12

During one summer I went on a mission trip to Ghana, Africa. It was a life-changing trip, but it was not easy. In the middle of the trip the leaders decided they were going to take us up into the Northern Mountain villages to minister. As we were driving to the villages, they told us we were going to be dropped off two by two at different villages to spend the night and minister the following day. Inside I was freaking out! Then they told me that I was being dropped off with the youngest girl on our trip who had never been on missions before! As I began to pray in tongues, I thought, *What am I doing here?*

As the bus drove away, I tried to be brave even though my heart was pounding in my ears. I met the pastors of the church and immediately they asked me to preach in their church service the next morning. I had never preached a full sermon before! Then they told me the service lasted four hours!

LIVE ON PURPOSE

Don't let anything hold you back from your call. It's not your age that's important; it's your relationship with God.

That night during dinner, which was some sort of grass soup I swallowed down, I wondered what I would speak on the next day. It got dark quickly, and I crawled into my mosquito net, lay on the mat on the ground, and tried to sleep. I tossed and turned as I tried to think about what to speak on the next day.

Then God spoke a verse to my heart from Jeremiah 1:6. In that verse Jeremiah said to God, "But Lord, I cannot speak, I am a youth! But God said, "'Do not say I am only a youth, for you will go to the people I send you and whatever I tell you, you will speak, do not be afraid of their faces for I am with you to deliver you,' says the Lord." God began to show me in His Word what I was to speak on the next day.

PRAYER

Father, even though I may be young and unqualified, I trust You to give me Your favor and ability for what You've called me to do. In ministry, in school, in my career, thank You for giving me Your provision, in Jesus' name.

No Fear, Part 2

For God did not give us a spirit of timidity (of cowardice, of craven and cringing and fawning fear), but [He has given us a spirit] of power and of love and of calm and well-balanced mind and discipline and self-control.

2 TIMOTHY 1:7 AMP

Just as I started to drift off to sleep, I began to hear the sound of bongo drums beating. They got louder and then I heard people chanting. We had been told that some of the people in Africa called upon evil spirits. Fear began to try to grip me. Then God's Word came to my heart from 2 Timothy 1:7 which says that God has not given me a spirit of fear but of power, love, and a sound mind. That night all that had been implanted in my heart over the years I have been a Christian came out. I bound that spirit of fear, pleaded the blood of Jesus, and declared His angels' protection over me.

The devil will do whatever he can to get you to cower in fear so you won't do what God wants you to do. But

LIVE ON PURPOSE

There is nothing like living in the Spirit, trusting God every day to deliver you. But the enemy will fight to keep you quiet and his weapon is fear. He knows that your faith in God will destroy him. Don't be fooled. With God nothing is impossible!

don't let the enemy intimidate you! Jesus Christ lives in you! Greater is He that is in you than he that is in the world (1 John 4:4).

When I woke up the next morning I felt butterflies in my stomach, but I continued to speak the Word over myself. When it was my time to speak, the Lord gave me the words to say. People got healed and saved! After the service the minister told me that the message I spoke to them was exactly what their congregation needed.

Fear comes in all shapes and sizes. Yet you cannot allow the spirit of fear to keep you from fulfilling your destiny. Step out today! Do something you have never done before and you will see things you have never seen before. Remember, God is with you!

PRAYER

Father God, in Jesus' name, I bind the spirit of fear from my life. God gave me a spirit of love, power, and a sound mind. I make my decisions and my judgments based on God's leading inside of me and His Word, not by the fear of man or any other thing.

A Good Thing

Who can find a virtuous wife?
For her wealth is far above rubies.

PROVERBS 31:10

"Hey." As I put my books down on my desk before class, a pleasant voice calmly asked for attention. "I saw your band the other night," she said matter-of-factly. I kept my cool, not wanting her to know that I was hanging on every word. What would she say?

The beautiful girl who was talking to me was, in fact, the woman of my dreams. I had been in class with her for a few weeks and had carefully observed her interaction with people. I watched how she reacted to guys who unabashedly flirted with her. I noted how diligent she was with her work. She seemed to treat everyone with the same openness. What confidence!

For the eighteen months previous, I had received more unsolicited attention from pretty girls than I ever had before. I was the singer in a rock band that had gained some notice on our Christian college campus. Beautiful girls had openly showed interest in me after hearing our band. I did not pursue them.

Ruth, the aforementioned beauty, was different. I invited her to come see our band perform. I thought maybe she would instantly fall in love with me, or something...we could just go from there.

Her actual response to seeing me perform was underwhelming. "You guys were pretty good." Her delivery was perfectly medium, somewhere between apathy and muted enthusiasm. I was staggered.

Ruth didn't play flirty games. I was impressed. After our brief conversation, I was convinced that I had found a woman of virtue!

LIVE ON PURPOSE TODAY

Read about "the virtuous woman" in Proverbs 31:10-31. Set your standards according to the Word today.

In our world young ladies are taught that they need to make themselves noticeable in order to find love. Revealing clothes and a flirtatious attitude are supposed to help them get what they want in life.

The Bible sets a higher standard for young ladies to find love. The goal is not to be *seen* as much as it is to be *found*. "Who can *find* a virtuous wife?" Virtue is a treasure worth finding.

I began to pursue Ruth because she was virtuous. I was very attracted to her physically, but it wasn't until I realized her true virtue that I seriously began to pursue her. Almost three years later, I married her.

PRAYER

Lord God, prepare me for my future spouse. Help me to remain pure until that day comes. In Jesus' name, amen.

Patmos

Being confident of this very thing, that he who has begun a good work in you will complete it until the day of Christ.

PHILIPPIANS 1:6

P atmos. A volcanic island in the middle of the Aegean Sea. Ten miles long by six miles wide, it was a tiny place to live with very little vegetation. Still, many people were shipped to this desolate island.

Although it may sound like the setting for the popular television show *Survivor,* this was an altogether different kind of reality. The people who were taken to Patmos were Roman prisoners.

As they crossed the 60 miles of sea from Ephesus, each prisoner was relegated to thoughts of life's end. Unlike the famous American island prison, Alcatraz, if someone attempted to escape Patmos, there was no place to swim.

During a time of tremendous persecution of Christians, the apostle John was banished to Patmos. It is likely that John had to work the granite quarries along with the rest of the colony of prisoners.

Here was a man who had walked with Jesus personally. Not only had he been one of Jesus' disciples, he was in the "inner circle" and was even called "the disciple whom Jesus loved."

But now, John was a lowly prisoner in exile. After having held such a place of honor, he had nothing to prove in ministry. Why didn't he wait out this wave of Christian persecution? Couldn't he have kept quite for a season? Instead, John's faithful witness led to his exile.

But Jesus had not abandoned John. It was here on the island of Patmos that God would speak to him in a marvelous way. John had taken time to worship God on "the Lord's day." As he was spending time with God, he heard "a loud voice as of a trumpet" behind him.

Jesus, Himself, appeared to John on that island! He gave John specific instructions to write down in a book. John wrote down everything he heard Jesus say. His writings became the book of Revelation.

John had lived a long life, and his ministry was full of great works. But it was not yet finished. Even on a desperate island, John was able to be an effective minister of the Gospel. God was faithful to complete His work in John to the end.

LIVE ON PURPOSE TODAY

Philippians 1:6, James 1:12, and Hebrews 12:1-2. Write out these Scriptures on note cards. Meditate on them today.

No matter what our circumstances look like in this life, as long as we are obedient to God, He will turn our obstacles into opportunities for His power to shine.

PRAYER

Father, I pray that You continue to lead me according to Your will. Thank You for Your faithfulness to me. In Jesus' name, amen.

Sharp Friends

As iron sharpens iron, so a man sharpens the countenance of his friend.

PROVERBS 27:17

Of Samuel and Susanna Wesley's 19 children, John and Charles were two of the youngest. John was a few years older than Charles; nevertheless, they had a close relationship.

By age 26, John had long since graduated from Oxford and was an ordained minister in the Anglican Church, following his father's footsteps. However, when Charles began to attend Oxford, John returned to the college scene.

John became a sort of spiritual advisor for several students, including his younger brother. As a deep hunger for the Word of God grew on the inside of them, these young men disciplined themselves and each other to study the Bible and spend time with God.

Their peers noticed the fervor John, Charles, and their friends had for the things of God. They ridiculed them, calling them "The Holy Club" or "methodists" for the methodical way in which they went about their devotion.

But in this time, John's and Charles' relationship with God became very personal to them. Inspired by Scripture, they began to imagine all of the good works they could do for people. There, in the formative years of their lives, a dream was conceived.

LIVE ON PURPOSE TODAY

Consider the people in your world who you could likely sharpen and be sharpened by. Pursue those relationships.

Before long, they found themselves leading people to Christ by the hundreds. Together they began to do great works for God: helping the poor with loan funds, establishing homes for widows and orphans, ministering to the imprisoned, reaching out to the military, and helping to provide medicine for the sick.

Before John Wesley was finished with his ministry, he had traveled over 250,000 miles and preached over 40,000 sermons. Charles Wesley had a heart for worship, writing some 7,000 hymns; many of which Christians still treasure today.

The ideas that had come from the devotion time of these two brothers had begun a movement that would influence the world. John and Charles Wesley are the founders of the Methodist Church.

It is of vital importance that you and I keep company with people of excellence. At an early age, John and Charles Wesley surrounded themselves with people who had a hunger for the things of God. You and I should do the same.

PRAYER

Father God, I thank You that You order my steps and bring me in the company of great men. In Jesus' name, amen.

Manners Matter

*Better is a dry morsel with quietness, than
a house full of feasting with strife.*

PROVERBS 17:1

In college I made friends with quite a few international students. One such friend, also named Stephen, had been reared in an affluent home in South Africa.

One afternoon Stephen and I were eating lunch together when the subject of manners came up. "I would say that you are the most well-mannered American I've met," he said. This was quite a compliment. Stephen reminded me of a young Hugh Grant, as polished and polite as British royalty.

Twenty years earlier, the odds would have been against someone ever making such a statement about me. My family's economic status was on the decline. We were barely getting by. It was one of the most difficult times in the life of our young family.

Determined to live within their means, but above expectations, my parents implemented something revolutionary to our home: "restaurant night." We couldn't afford to go to a real restaurant, but that's not what "restaurant night" was about.

Friday nights, Mom and Dad would prepare a special meal, while the kids dressed in our nicest clothes. When the meal was ready, we would all sit down together at the dining room table.

LIVE ON PURPOSE TODAY

Begin elevating your manners and etiquette today.

There we saw the setting of Mom's nice tableware. In a matter of moments we be served the special meal of the night. Even with something as simple as hamburgers, they would always go the extra mile. A Superman "S" was drawn with ketchup and mustard on the bun and "Clark Kent" glasses (two pickles and toothpicks) were on the burger.

In this setting, we were taught how to have good manners and etiquette at the dinner table. Eventually, we caught on.

We never considered the fact that we were too poor to have such refined manners. My parents had their hopes set on the future. They realized that our present circumstances were temporary. They taught us how to have good manners and etiquette long before it ever looked like we would need them.

What does having manners have to do with our spiritual lives? Good manners and etiquette are not about economic class or ethnicity. They are about displaying self-control and deference to others, both of which are attributes of Christ.

The details of how we live make impressions on people for good or bad. If we bear the name of Christ, as Christians, shouldn't we strive to put our best foot forward?

PRAYER

Father God, I thank You that You love me for who I am and lead me towards who You want me to be. In Jesus' name, amen.

Patrick's Revenge

Patrick knew what it was like to be used. He was a slave in a foreign country. When he was 16, pirates raided his home in Britain and captured him, selling him to an Irish chieftain!

Patrick had been raised in a Christian home. His father was a well-respected man with strong beliefs. When Patrick found himself in these dreadful circumstances, he had a choice to make. He could blame God for what had happened, or he could run to God for help.

Patrick chose the latter and resolved to grow closer to God in this desperate time. After six years he escaped and made his way back home to England.

There, again, Patrick had a choice to make. He had a right to hold a grudge against these people who had stolen a major part of his life. Instead, Patrick had compassion on them.

For the next several years, Patrick devoted himself to the Scriptures. He submitted himself to the wisdom of church leaders, vowing to someday take the gospel back to Ireland, the land of the people who had been his enemy.

Finally, Patrick launched out into missionary work to the people of northern and western Ireland. This people group had never heard the gospel!

Patrick used his knowledge of the tribal culture and quickly gained the trust of many tribal leaders. This influence enabled him to lead several people to Christ. Before he was done, it is said that Patrick formed more than 300 churches and baptized some 120,000 new Irish believers.

In the most critical times of his life, Patrick chose to have a tender heart before God. Because of this, God was able to

LIVE ON PURPOSE TODAY

Surprise that person who is hateful towards you by doing something good for him today.

use Patrick to change an entire nation, winning thousands of souls. Even today, Irish people all over the world celebrate St. Patrick's Day, in honor of Patrick.

It is highly unlikely that you will ever have pirates raid your city, capture you, and sell you into slavery. But certainly all of us have people in our lives who are hateful towards us.

Jesus introduced a revolutionary idea to His disciples: "Pray for those who spitefully use you and persecute you." This concept deals not only with our actions, but also the condition of our hearts. If we can do good for those who are our enemies, the love of God will compel them to come to Christ.

PRAYER

Father God, I pray that You soften the hearts of those who wish me ill will. Show them Your love through me. In Jesus' name, amen.

Dodge the Ditches

One warm summer afternoon, I got a call that some friends were going to play softball, and they asked me to join them. There wasn't a whole lot else to do at the time, so I was thrilled at the opportunity.

I jumped in my '66 Ford Mustang and headed down the street towards our high school baseball field, which was less than a mile away. I loved my car. It was almost 30 years old, but it was a classic.

Sure, it had its faults. There was a hole in the floorboard through which you could see the street below. The air conditioning didn't work and it had no power steering, to name a few.

On this short journey, though, one of these imperfections distracted me more than it should have. Not having air conditioning, I tried to roll down the driver-side window as I was driving.

Oh yeah, there were no power windows in this beautiful machine either. So, I had to roll my window down, now get this…manually. You may have never even seen a vehicle without electric windows, but they did exist at one time.

So, as I manually rolled down my window, it came off track, meaning it would no longer roll down or up. It was stuck. This had happened before, so I knew just what to do.

I took one hand to push down on the top of the window, rotated the handle with my other hand, and steered with my knee. The window was stuck worse than usual, so I was more distracted than usual. Finally it budged, but when I looked up, I realized I was about to run off the road!

LIVE ON PURPOSE TODAY

Identify the distractions in your life. Move on from them today.

I slammed on the brakes, but it was too late. My

front right tire had already gone over the edge. As I skid to a halt, I found myself in an awkward predicament.

The Mustang was teetering over a ditch and I was stuck! The front wheel on the passenger's side was hanging out in thin air. I was not even one block from my house, so shortly thereafter, my brother and my dad helped me pull the car out, laughing all the way.

When you and I set out to reach our goals in life, there are many distractions that try to derail us from our true path. If we take our eyes off of our destination, we will find ourselves in the awkward and embarrassing position of being stuck in the ditches of life.

PRAYER

Father God, thank You that my steps are ordered.
Enable me to keep my focus on You. In Jesus' name, amen.

Think Big

For as the heavens are higher than the earth,
so are my ways higher than your ways,
and my thoughts than your thoughts.

ISAIAH 55:9

The young ruler must have been flooded with thoughts of wonder as he considered the great task before him. His father had been a great king, loved by the people. Now Solomon was charged with the task of leading his nation.

At the beginning of his reign as king, Solomon worshipped God with a sacrifice in a place called Gibeon. That night, the pre-incarnate Christ appeared to Solomon and said, "Ask! What shall I give you?"

This was a moment of truth for Solomon. What he asked of God in this moment would set the tone for his reign as king. He could have asked for any number of things, but he asked for understanding.

Solomon knew that if he were to be a great leader, he would have to think bigger. God was well pleased with Solomon's request. In time, God gave Solomon more wisdom and understanding than any man who had ever lived.

Solomon was faithful to go through the process of expanding his understanding. He was able to broaden his perspective and think the thoughts of God. He began to have understanding of the ways of God.

Soon Solomon commissioned a labor force of close to 200,000 men to build God's temple, a place worthy to house the Ark of the Covenant.

After many years of hard work, Solomon finished the temple, accomplishing what even his father David couldn't. He had built the temple that David dreamed of. Word of Solomon's excellence spread throughout the world.

The queen of Sheba was one of the first to come and behold all that

LIVE ON PURPOSE TODAY

Think big! Seek God's wisdom and understanding in every situation in your life today.

God had done through Solomon. She traveled about 1200 miles to Jerusalem, and the Bible tells us that when she had seen Solomon's wisdom, the house that he had built, the food on his table, the excellence of his servants, waiters, and cupbearers, she fainted.

Solomon soon surpassed all the kings of the earth in riches and wisdom. His fame spread throughout the world until everyone wanted to hear his wisdom.

Solomon would never have reached that point as a king had he not recognized his need to think bigger. He knew his understanding was limited. If he were going to succeed in life, he needed God's thoughts.

PRAYER

*Father God, I thank You for giving wisdom freely
to those who ask. So, give me wisdom and
understanding I pray. In Jesus' name, amen.*

Factoring Out Fear

For God hath not given us the spirit of fear;
but of power, and of love, and of a sound mind.

2 TIMOTHY 1:7

When I was about six years old, I had horrifying nightmares. They were the kind of nightmares that would have scared any full-grown adult, so as a kindergartener, it's a wonder I ever went to sleep at night.

When I woke up from these nightmares, I was too petrified to move. So, I would just lie there in the dark, sweat dripping down my back, the hairs on my neck standing up. After several minutes I would get up the courage to yell out "Maaamma!"

Mom knew about the nightmares, so she would put on her nightgown and come down to see me. Soon I would have peace as she taught me how to speak God's Word in those times.

The nightmares stopped after a couple of years, but I never forgot them. Because I was in the dark when I had these nightmares, even when I became a teenager, I feared the dark.

There were nights when I would have to go alone to my dad's church to pick something up for him. In that old creaky church, the light switches were a long way from the door.

On one such trip, as I walked down the middle aisle of the sanctuary in pitch-black darkness, fear gripped me. My heart started pounding. I began to imagine that vagrants were sleeping in the pews, ready to jump out at me at any moment. I got so scared that I stopped right in the middle of the sanctuary, eyes wide-opened.

LIVE ON PURPOSE TODAY

Identify any areas of your life in which you have fear. Begin speaking the Word over those areas today!

But then something rose up within me. I realized the absurdity of battling this fear, yet I was still petrified. So, I shouted at the top of my lungs, "God has not given me a spirit of fear, but of love and power and a sound mind!"

Wow, that really helped, I thought. So I did it again… and again. Each time, the fear loosened its grip more and more, until it was not there!

That night, I chose to overcome fear, and I never feared the dark again. Fear can affect you in many areas of your life. So give no place to it nor allow it to keep you from experiencing the fullness of what God has for you.

PRAYER

Lord Jesus, I thank You that I don't have to give place to fear in my life. You've empowered me with faith today. In Jesus' name, amen.

Standing Strong

In high school I worked on a televised A.M. program with several other students. On one occasion, my co-host remarked about a comment in the school newspaper: "The newspaper said that we look tired on the air and wear bags under our eyes like an accessory. They don't realize that we have to get up at 6 A.M. in the morning to get here on time!"

The national/international newsman agreed. "Yeah, I don't think the newspaper has a right to say anything until they mop up the misspellings in their articles."

My co-host turned back to me. "What do you have to say about it, Trecie?"

Underneath the glare of hot white lights, I had a decision to make. Either I could engage in rebutting the newspaper's remarks (besides, they had made some pretty nasty comments about us), or I could keep my peace and hold my tongue. Just when I was about to rip the newspaper department to shreds, the Holy Spirit arrested me with Ephesians 4:29:

Let no corrupt communication proceed out of your mouth; but that which is good to the use of edifying, that it may minister grace unto the hearers.

Even though the hosts had not cursed, the communication was not edifying to the newspaper department. In this case, there were over 3000 "hearers"—students and faculty—waiting with bated breath for my response.

"No comment," I replied simply.

Just two words, but they spoke volumes. At the end of the broadcast, I said, "The A.M. cast and crew will take all comments from the newspaper into consideration."

My decision may not have won ratings, but it won

LIVE ON PURPOSE

As you allow the Holy Spirit to lead you in everyday decisions, He can begin to bring greater opportunities across your path.

God's approval. And in the end, His opinion is the only one that matters.

PRAYER

Father God, I ask You to help me today to make right decisions. When I am tempted to go along with other people who are not following Your ways, I'm asking that You give me Your resolve to stand strong for what's right, in Jesus' name.

Astronomical Design

When I consider Your heavens, the work of Your fingers,
the moon and the stars, which You have ordained,
what is man that You are mindful of him?

PSALM 8:3,4

O rder. Design. Purpose. These words can be used to describe the created world in which we live. The sun rises and sets right on time every day. The ocean's tide comes in and goes out.

Even those who study the heavens can see the order, design, and purpose of God. The sun, the other planets in our solar system, and even our moon are all set at a perfect distance from Earth, without which life could not exist.

When King David looked into the heavens, he wrote, "When I consider Your heavens, the work of Your fingers, the moon and the stars, which You have ordained, what is man that You are mindful of him?" Ordained? How so?

Some scholars say that there is such order to God's creation, that even the stars tell the gospel story. Two thousand years ago, the Magi (we know them as kings or wise men) were so convinced of this that they left their homes and country to follow an evanescent star that they believed pointed to the Messiah.

Was this just a fabulous story, or is there scientific documentation of this star? It so happens that astronomers concur that such a star did appear in the night sky at that time in history.

LIVE ON PURPOSE TODAY

Bring order to any chaotic area of your life today. See how God blesses you for it!

Although it appeared to be one bright star, the wise men had likely seen an astronomical occurrence that only happens every 800 years. The planets Mars, Jupiter, and Saturn aligned themselves in the constellation of Pisces, creating a beautiful spectacle in the heavens, which looked like a brilliant star.

The wise men were able to follow this "star" because the occurrence happened three times that year! When they found Jesus, they worshipped Him, giving Him gifts from their country: gold, frankincense, and myrrh. These Gentile men had seen God's order, design, and purpose in the heavens and recognized that it all pointed to a Savior.

We, too, are a part of God's creation. The hairs of our heads are numbered, our thoughts are known, the steps of those who follow Him are ordered.

God has a beautiful design and purpose for you! If you will continue to keep Jesus as the center focus of your existence, you will experience the wonder of God's order, design, and purpose in your life.

PRAYER

Father God, I submit my life to You wholly. Thank You for being mindful of me. In Jesus' name, amen.

Disneyland Bound

When I was a toddler, my dad would go on long trips for work from time to time. His job was to drive charter buses for businesses in the Phoenix area.

He was often going to exciting places. Of course, at age four, the thought of going on any kind of special trip with my dad was thrilling. I'm sure there were many times when I begged to be able to go with him. Understandably, most of the time, he had to say no.

One time, however, I heard Mom mention that Dad was about to take a trip to Disneyland! This was far too wonderful for my four-year-old mind to fathom. I pleaded with my mom to let me go. "Momma, can I pleeeeease go?"

Mom's reply was interesting. "You'll have to ask your father." Most of the time Mom referred to Dad as "your daddy," so when she responded this way, I misunderstood. I dropped to my knees and closed my eyes. "Heavenly Father, can I please go to Disneyland?" This innocent mistake made such an impression on my parents that they somehow found a way for me to go.

Why do we refer to God as our heavenly Father? Isn't Jesus God's "only begotten Son"? Well, the Bible tells us that when we accept Jesus into our hearts, we become "children of God" and "joint heirs with Christ."

This speaks to the relationship we have with God. We are not like the rest of His creation. We are not just servants of God. He is our *Father.* We were meant to commune with Him.

When we come to Him, we should do so as freely as a dependent child approaches a loving father. In fact, Jesus reflected that attitude in His ministry, saying, "Whoever does not receive the kingdom of God as a little child, will by no means enter it."

LIVE ON PURPOSE TODAY

If you don't ask, you won't receive. So, ask your heavenly Father for the desires of your heart today!

Just as I audaciously asked my parents to let me go to Disneyland, God wants us to ask of Him freely. God is looking for people who approach Him with that kind of faith.

PRAYER

Dear God, I thank You that You loved me enough to bring me into Your family. Thank You that I can call on You as my Father. In Jesus' name, amen.

Haydn's Hiatus

Be angry, and do not sin. Meditate within your heart on your bed, and be still.

PSALM 4:4

Joseph Haydn was a promising young musician in the 1700's when he landed a job with the Esterhazy family. The Esterhazys were prosperous Hungarian royalty. Haydn's job was to create most of the music for the Esterhazy court.

He was just 29 when he started but would spend the next 30 years of his life working for this family. There he wrote several symphonies and operas.

Without a doubt, Haydn's works continued to improve as he aged. But Haydn learned another art form during his employ with the Esterhazys, the art of confrontation.

As the story goes, Haydn and the other musicians of the household were overworked. A vacation was well deserved and much needed, but it seemed Prince Nikolaus Esterhazy had not even considered it.

It would have been understandable for Haydn to expeditiously approach Prince Nikolaus to demand a recess. It would have been understandable for Haydn and his cohorts to go on some sort of strike, but they didn't.

LIVE ON PURPOSE TODAY

Write down the top three issues that irk you right now. Creatively consider ways to confront these issues.

Haydn valued his relationship with the family. After all, they had been good to him for several years. Instead of filing a complaint, Haydn composed a new symphony. In order to get his message across with a certain amount of discretion, Haydn had a plan.

At symphony's end, one by one, certain instruments would tastefully drop out. As each individual musician stopped playing, he would stand up and walk off stage until one lone musician remained to finish the symphony.

Prince Nikolaus discerned the message. Haydn and the rest were promptly given a vacation. Haydn had successfully confronted the issue in a charming way that perhaps even enhanced his relationship with the good prince.

Confrontation is a lost art form today. Many people are not able to detach the issues that anger them from the people involved. Therefore, some people confront in a mean-spirited way, while others allow issues to fester, not confronting them at all.

As Christians, you and I need to know how to confront issues while protecting the dignity of the people we confront. The Scriptures don't tell us that we should ignore the issues. In fact, the Bible says, "Be angry, and do not sin."

Haydn's story illustrates this principle beautifully. He did not *react* to the issue at hand; rather, after much consideration, he *responded*.

PRAYER

*Lord Jesus, I thank You that You have enabled
me to confront the issues in my life with
Your wisdom. In Jesus' name, amen.*

Influence

{ *Let your light so shine before men, that they may see your good works and glorify your Father in heaven.* }

MATTHEW 5:16

"**W**ell, just forget it!" I exclaimed. "I guess I shouldn't have cast my pearls before swine!" "What?" he said. "Did you just call me swine?" "No, wait, that's not what I meant..." I started to say, but it was too late.

That was roughly how one of my first teenage witnessing experiences ended. It was awful. I had tried to explain deep theological truths to someone I barely knew. When he didn't get it, I lost my patience and lashed out at him.

Here was a guy who had come to befriend me and I rudely distanced myself from him. He wasn't a bad guy at all. To make matters worse, I really needed a friend. I was new in town, and this guy knew everybody!

When school started, everyone seemed to know his side of the story. This complicated my social life for a while. They all must have thought I was a self-righteous person.

God corrected me gently though. He helped me to see the mistake I had made. I had tried to witness to someone with whom I had no influence. Influence is the key to witnessing for Christ.

After a year and a half at that high school, I finally built up enough influence to make an impact. I was one of the starting basketball players on the varsity team. Soon I was known all over the area.

Since I was an athlete, I could identify with other athletes. I befriended two of our high school's top baseball players in one of my classes. One day I decided to invite them both to come with me to a Monday night Bible study for teens. What could it hurt to ask?

I knew full well that both of these guys had a history of drinking

LIVE ON PURPOSE TODAY

Write down a strategy to win influence with an unsaved friend. Start implementing your plan today.

and going to wild parties. They were hard cases. I wasn't sure what they would say. To my surprise, they both agreed to come!

That night at the Bible study, *both* of my friends bowed their heads, closed their eyes, and repented of their sins. *Both* guys asked Jesus into their hearts that night!

In gaining influence, I had identified with these two guys. They noticed how I lived, and when the time came, I cashed in on my influence in order to win them to Christ. Influence works.

PRAYER

Lord, show me ways to gain influence with unbelievers, compelling them to come to You. In Jesus' name, amen.

Mighty Mites

So let each one give as he purposes in his heart....

2 CORINTHIANS 9:7

She was in mourning. Her husband was deceased and she was left alone, a lowly widow pauper. That day, she made her way through a crowded temple.

Her goal was to offer up selfless worship to God with discretion. Had she known that any set of eyes had been fixed upon her, she would have been too embarrassed to continue.

She must have passed several people as they gave their sum to the treasury boxes. Many wealthy people must have demonstratively contributed large sums all around her. Yet she pushed past all of them, pursuant of a discrete place to offer her own gift.

Her gift was the lowest lawful gift, yet it was all she had to live on that day. Little did she know, the sound of those two coins hitting the bottom of the temple treasury box would echo throughout eternity.

Jesus Christ had set His gaze upon her actions that day. He had likely taken His disciples to steps that overlooked the temple. There they had seen many people giving large sums.

Jesus pointed out this woman to them as an example. He preserved her dignity by not doing it in front of her. "This poor woman has put in more than all those who have given to the treasury; for they all put in out of their abundance, but she out of her poverty put in all she had...."

It wasn't that Christ was displeased with the gifts of the others. He was moved by the gift of this woman because it showed her complete trust in God to take care of her needs.

Many people cling to the little they have when money gets tight. They become so fearful of what might happen if

LIVE ON PURPOSE TODAY

Ask God to show you ways to give to His work consistently.

they lose what little they have, that the idea of giving a portion of it away is almost unthinkable to them.

God wants us to give to Him as an act of worship and surrender. It is a way of recognizing our utter dependence upon Him.

The Psalmist exclaimed, "The earth is the Lord's and all its fullness." It all belongs to God. He doesn't want us to give so that we stay poor. On the contrary, as we worship God with our giving, it enables Him to bless us beyond what we could ask or think.

PRAYER

Father in heaven, I thank You for all You've
provided for me. I purpose to worship You
with my giving. In Jesus' name, amen.

Fly, Fly Again

Your young men shall see visions.

JOEL 2:28

A young man named Jason moved to the United States from South Africa in the early 1990's. Here in the States, McDonald would start the process of becoming a U.S. citizen.

Although he was just a teenager, McDonald's vision for his life was firmly in place. He loved his new country and fully intended on helping defend her as a pilot in the United States Navy someday. But that dream seemed like it would never come to pass.

From the start, Jason faced many obstacles that would hinder his accomplishing this vision. The first obstacle was his citizenship. He couldn't sign up to serve a nation in which he wasn't a citizen! This was going to take time.

Before he could become a citizen, like most people transplanted to the U.S. from foreign soil, Jason had to spend a few years establishing himself. This delay didn't deter him from the vision though.

McDonald enrolled in college so that when he was eventually able to join the Navy, he would come in as an officer. Meanwhile, much of his spare time was devoted to flying. He logged several hours as a pilot, flying small private planes.

He spent hours and hours playing flight simulation computer and video games. He watched movies and television shows that featured aircrafts of all different kinds.

These things I saw firsthand. Jason was my roommate in college. I saw his unwavering dedication to the vision. I saw him work tirelessly, pressing on towards the realization of his dream.

LIVE ON PURPOSE TODAY

Write down your vision for this year. See how God helps you accomplish it!

After college, Jason finally became eligible for United States citizenship. By this time, he had long since developed relationships with Navy recruiters.

When all the perfunctory paperwork was done, McDonald started right away.

It didn't take long for the Navy to catch on. Jason's vision was clear. Within a short time, he had passed the rigorous tests and training. After years of focused effort, Jason finally accomplished his vision of becoming a pilot for the United States Navy.

Few people seem to latch on to a life's vision so early on in life as Jason did. Some, in fact, never identify their God-given desires in the first place. Such people wander around aimlessly, never experiencing the fulfillment of living out their dreams.

Without vision, you will never serve God's purpose for your life. So begin to seek God right now. He will give you a great vision for your life!

PRAYER

Father God, help me to focus in on the vision You have placed inside of me. In Jesus' name, amen.

Faith for Small Things

But without faith it is impossible to please him:
for he that cometh to God must believe that he is, and
that he is a rewarder of them that diligently seek him.

HEBREWS 11:6 KJV

L ast summer while visiting my family, my aunt pulled out lots of old pictures for us to look at, and to my delight, I saw that she had some school pictures of both my siblings and me. This was quite surprising for me because my family had a house fire that destroyed our childhood pictures.

Later that afternoon my sister went to a store to make copies of our pictures. She wasn't able to make the copies and when she returned home, my little picture was missing. Well, right then I put my foot down and said, "No, it is not lost." I prayed that God would show me where it was. I called the store and asked if they had found the tiny picture. The answer was "no." Later that evening I went to the store to look for myself. I had the cleaning crew called and still the answer was "no." I began to walk the aisles of the store and pray. After about 40 minutes with no success, I started heading toward the door. All of the sudden I heard over the intercom, "Would the lady who's looking for a school picture, please come to the photography area?" I ran over and there stood a man over six feet tall with the picture in hand!

This man felt that God told him to go through nearly three feet of trash, piece by piece, and with liquid all through it. At the very bottom of the trash he found it, and it was in spotless condition. He told me that he was a Christian and he felt in his heart that he needed to look as thoroughly as he could. I told him that I was a Christian and that God had used his obedience to

LIVE ON PURPOSE

God will honor your faith even in small things. Your well-being is very important to Him. Take time to put your faith in God for big and small things.

answer my prayer. He was so blessed that God had used him, and so was I!

PRAYER

Father, I will believe You to help me in small things and big things. You are pleased when I release my faith and trust You to bring those things into my life. I purpose in my heart to bring these issues to You instead of trying to do them in my own strength, in Jesus' name.

In Your Hands

For I wish that all men were even as myself.
But each one has his own gift from God,
one in this manner and another in that.

1 CORINTHIANS 7:7

In the late 1980's, my favorite athlete was John Elway, the quarterback of the Denver Broncos. Elway was a master at the fourth quarter comeback. If the Broncos were ever down in a close game, you could always count on Elway to somehow lead the team to victory.

In both 1987 and 1988 Elway took the Broncos to the Super Bowl. Even though they lost both games, the Broncos remained my favorite team and Elway my favorite player.

Christmas day, 1988, my brother and I received a very special gift. It was an actual NFL football! We were thrilled. But not only was it an NFL regulation football, it was one of the practice balls that the Denver Broncos used!

We inflated it right away and began to toss it around the yard. All of a sudden we realized that there was a possibility John Elway himself, one of the greatest quarterbacks who ever lived, may have held this very football in his hands. John Elway may have passed this ball around in practice!

From that point on, we threw that football with a new sense of confidence. It was as if the greatness of John Elway would somehow rub off on us. If only it were so.

In our hands it was just another hunk of inflated leather. In the hands of John Elway, however, that hunk of leather represented sheer greatness.

God Almighty has placed a unique gift into your hands. You alone can take that gift and make something great of it, but you must cultivate it. If you try to make someone else's gift work for you, it probably won't. Likewise, your gift in someone else's hands is futile.

LIVE ON PURPOSE TODAY

Write down five things you're not good at and five things you are good at. See if that helps you identify your gifts.

The more you can identify the gift God has put into your hands, the more useful that gift becomes. The harder you work to develop that gift, the closer you will come to fulfilling God's unique call on your life with excellence.

PRAYER

*God in heaven, I pray for Your guidance as
I identify the unique gifts You have given me. I purpose
to use them for Your glory. In Jesus' name, amen.*

At Your Word

{ *Nevertheless, at Your word I will let down the net....*

LUKE 5:5 }

Certainly there was guesswork involved in the profession. In tracking down live animals of any kind, there must have been several variables to consider. Especially as a fisherman, determining the best place and time to throw out the nets was crucial. Of all the points of conjecture, however, it was a commonly shared belief amongst real fishermen that the best time to fish was at night.

One morning, after an embarrassingly unsuccessful night of fishing, a man named Simon and his blue-collar fishing crew were ashore cleaning their nets as a large crowd approached. It was evident that the people were there to hear one man teach.

Simon allowed the man to board his boat so that the people could hear what He had to say. This man was Jesus of Nazareth. There, on that boat, Jesus sat down and taught the crowds of people.

After He was finished, Jesus had one request of Simon, who had also heard Him speak. He requested that Simon launch his boat out one more time and let his nets down for a catch.

It must have taken every bit of decency Simon had not to roll his eyes and reject this request. Sure, Jesus was a great teacher, but when it came to fishing, Simon was the professional.

But in Simon's answer, we see something most notable. "Master, we have toiled all night and caught nothing; nevertheless at Your word, I will let down the net." Those middle few words, "at Your word, I will...," were powerful. They released faith that opened the door for a miracle.

As Simon and his crew cast their nets, they hit full payload! To their amazement,

LIVE ON PURPOSE TODAY

Find good teachers of the Word. Listen to their tapes or radio programs, or watch them on television regularly.

they had landed the catch of all catches. There were so many fish in that one catch that it filled up two full boats!

Simon and his partners were astonished with what Jesus had done. From that point forward, they left everything to follow Him.

"At Your word, I will...." A life devoted to Christ begins with those few words. Surrendering our own will to the will of God is just the first step. If we are going to know God and experience the fullness of a relationship with Him, we must take Him at His Word.

The Word of God is the revelation of the will of God for each of us. So stay tuned in to God's Word and live it!

PRAYER

Lord Jesus, I will obey Your Word. Teach me
Your ways, I pray. In Jesus' name, amen.

Sharpen Your Work

> *If the ax is dull, and one does not sharpen the edge, then he must use more strength; But wisdom brings success.*
>
> ECCLESIASTES 10:10

I was snowed in and I wasn't fully prepared for it. Sure we had enough water and food for several days, but that wasn't enough for me.

I'm a person of action. I need some kind of physical activity from time to time. That's why I love sports so much. But being snowed in, there wasn't a whole lot I could do.

Since the condo we lived in was evidently built before box springs were invented, the stairs leading to the second floor were designed in such a way that it was impossible for us to get the box spring for our queen-sized bed up to the second floor. So for the first few weeks of our marriage, Ruth and I slept on a mattress, with no box spring.

Snowed in, box spring stuck downstairs, need for physical activity—combustible. I decided that it was high time for me to do something about the box spring situation. My plan: saw the wooden braces in half, fold the box spring, negotiate the box spring up the stairway, repair the wood braces, and set the box spring up for use.

Not a bad plan in theory. The only problem, I didn't have a saw! And I was snowed in! Determined not to capitulate, I went on with my plan.

Instead of a saw, I used a steak knife. That's right, a steak knife. I cut and cut and cut. Half an hour turned into an hour. One hour turned into two…and then three.

I willed my way through those lightweight wooden braces with the power of my steak knife. What would have taken less than five minutes with an electric saw, took me hours! If only I had used wisdom.

The Bible tells us that

LIVE ON PURPOSE TODAY

Take a moment to consider the various tasks you do at home, work, or school. Ask God to show you smarter ways to accomplish those tasks.

wisdom brings success. In other words, it's okay not to work as hard as you can. Yes, you read that right. Working hard is important, but not as important as working smart.

If we expend all of our energies on less effective methods in life, we will not go very far. Using wisdom allows us to use our energy in more effective ways, propelling us to ultimate success.

PRAYER

Father God, I pray that You enable me to see smarter ways to work in every task I set my hands to. In Jesus' name, amen.

Identification

One winter I was traveling across the state of Arkansas right after a winter storm had hit. The roads were covered with ice and snow. Every couple of miles or so, there were vehicles that had slipped off the sides of the road. Most vehicles on the road were cautiously traveling no faster than forty miles per hour.

Soon we approached Little Rock, Arkansas' largest city. Before we knew it we were stopped, stuck in the middle of wall-to-wall traffic. We still had several hours of travel ahead of us. The thought of being stuck in traffic for any amount of time was frustrating.

We turned on the radio to see if we could find out what the conditions were like ahead of us. One station invited people to call in to tell their stories of being stuck in traffic.

For several minutes we heard stories of people who had traveled our same road the night before. Traffic had backed up so much the night before that people had to sleep in their cars. One story after another, it was almost as if people found some kind of camaraderie with those who had experienced the same troubles that they did.

I finally crept my way to an exit and pulled into a gas station. Upon entering the restroom, I realized this was a special situation. There is an unwritten rule somewhere that guys just don't talk to one another in the restroom. Especially to strangers.

To my surprise, during my brief visit to the restroom, two guys struck up conversations with me about their travel woes on the icy roads. I walked back out into the conven- ient store and

LIVE ON PURPOSE TODAY

Make an effort to identify with someone in your world who doesn't know Christ today.

everyone was talking to one another! The fact that *everybody* was experiencing the same difficulties caused us all to let down our inhibitions.

This was a great example of identification. We could all identify with one another because of our common battle. We could actually empathize with one another because we were in it together.

Identification. It's why God sent Jesus to earth as a man. The Bible tells us that Christ was "tempted in all points as we are, yet without sin." He did that so that we could identify with Him.

Once we are able to identify with Christ, we see that we, too, can live as He lived and our hearts are open to receiving Him.

PRAYER

Dear Jesus, I thank You for loving me enough to identify with me. Help me to identify with those who don't know You. In Jesus' name, amen.

In the Process

As an eagle stirs up its nest, hovers over its young, spreading out its wings, taking them up, carrying them on its wings, so the Lord alone led (Moses).

DEUTERONOMY 32:11,12

It's not that they don't have wings yet. They do. It's not that they haven't seen their mother fly for their whole lives. They have. It's just that the eaglets themselves have never attempted to fly.

For 11 or 12 weeks, their mother has hunted down food for them so they could grow and develop in the safety of the nest. There in the nest, they have watched their mother take off and land over and over again. They have seen her soar.

By the end of 11 or 12 weeks, if the eaglets could talk, they would be able to give an analysis on "how all eagles ought to fly." Although they themselves have never tried it, they've seen it done. But trying provides a wonderful new perspective to doing.

In the height of their comfort, the mother eagle stirs up the nest. All of a sudden the eaglets are provoked to action. Mother eagle spreads her giant wings and elevates the eaglets from the nest in an instant.

She takes them high in the air, carrying them on her wings. Soon she will release them to fly on their own. They have seen it done so many times. Their wings are wide enough. Their bodies are big enough. Will they soar on their first try? Of course not.

LIVE ON PURPOSE TODAY

Ask God to reveal to you what your next step is in your spiritual maturation process.

In fact, they won't be able to fly very well at all. There is a process they must go through to really learn to fly. They'll make several mistakes in their first attempts. But mother eagle will be there to guide them.

They will not be able to hunt on their own for several months, but mother eagle will teach them how. The more they learn, the less involved she is in correction and instruction.

God leads us in this way. He nurtures and equips us. He gives us examples of how to live. And as we embark on a life devoted to Him, He gently corrects our mistakes. He feeds us until we can feed ourselves.

God's desire is that we reach a level of spiritual maturity, that we spend time in His Word daily. His desire is that we examine and correct ourselves. If we dedicate ourselves to His great process, we too will soar.

PRAYER

Father, I am open to the process You have for me.
Where You lead, I will follow. In Jesus' name, amen.

Running To Win

*Do you not know that those who run in
a race all run, but one receives the prize?
Run in such a way that you may obtain it.*

1 CORINTHIANS 9:24

"It's haaard, but it's fair!" shouted Coach Rufus as we huffed and puffed our way around the track for another lap. "It's haaard, but it's fair!"

Preseason conditioning. It was the part of high school basketball that we all hated. After months of "loafing," it was time to get our bodies back into shape. But that was only part of the purpose of preseason conditioning.

I surmised that Coach Rufus was not just watching to see who had natural speed. He wanted to weed out the quitters, and, most importantly, find out who had real heart and determination.

In previous seasons, I had been the slowest guy on the team. During conditioning, we were required to run the mile in under 6 minutes and 30 seconds in order to be eligible for tryouts. I barely made it.

This year I was determined not to be last. I set my sights on Derek, the fastest guy on the team. For distance runs, Derek probably ran at about 70 percent of his top speed. I had to run at about 85 percent to keep up.

After the first lap, I felt okay. Staying on pace with Derek built my confidence. Maybe I could keep up with him the whole way!

After a quarter mile I was still with him, but my lungs started to burn. I controlled my breathing so as not to let him know that I was tiring.

At the half-mile point, the burn was excruciating, but I kept pushing. Gasping for air now, there was no way I could hide my fatigue from Derek, but I stayed with it.

Soon, I began to contemplate slowing

LIVE ON PURPOSE TODAY

Read the victorious stories of 2-3 Bible characters you admire. Apply them to your life.

down. Finishing fourth or fifth out of fifteen would be better than last place. But with a quarter mile left to go, something happened.

To my surprise, Derek began to slow down. He had set a pace too fast even for himself to keep up. I still had some endurance left because I had been preparing for this day. I pushed past Derek, keeping the pace for the rest of the mile. I finished in 5 minutes and 49 seconds, first place!

Everyone was shocked, including me. I wasn't the fastest or the most athletic. I had just run the race in such a way that I might win.

As Christians, you and I should run the race of life to win. Just like in a physical race, self-denial and self-discipline are part of what it takes to push through to victory. If we stay faithful to God for the whole race, we win!

PRAYER

Lord God, I will remain faithful to You in my life.
Thank You for equipping me to win.

The Big Thank You

Oh give thanks to the Lord!

2 CHRONICLES 16:8

Just to see someone infected by this awful disease would have been horrifying, with visible parts of skin slowly deteriorating. Many times a nose or an ear would be gone, eaten away by the bacteria that caused this incurable disease.

Leprosy. The most feared disease of the day. It wasn't fatal, but it affected every aspect of life for those who contracted it.

Physically, if left untreated, it could be debilitating. Advanced cases would harm the eyes, the liver, and even the bones.

Socially, lepers were outcasts. No one wanted to see them. No one wanted to be touched by them. Fear motivated people to stay away.

Spiritually, they were considered "unclean." It was a commonly held misconception of the day that disease of any kind was caused by sin. Many of the lepers must have believed it.

This was a miserable existence. Lepers must have dreamed of ways to just get the disease to stop. One day, such a dream miraculously came true for ten lepers. However, not all of them received everything they could have.

By this time, stories of Jesus' miracles must have traveled all across the land. These lepers must have been heartened to hear that He was coming their way that day.

Although they had to stay at a distance, they waited for Him. When Jesus and His disciples finally passed their way, the lepers shouted out, "Jesus, Master, have mercy on us!"

Jesus gave them specific instructions. As they obeyed, their

LIVE ON PURPOSE TODAY

Whether today is a bad or good day, take a look at the good things in your life and say "thank You" to God!

dream came true. Leprosy ceased. No longer were they unclean outcasts. These ten men were given a miraculous gift from God. Yet only one of them did the right thing with their gift.

The one leper did what it took to find his way back to Jesus. With a loud voice he glorified God. Falling down on his face at the feet of Jesus, he said, "Thank You."

After simply saying "thanks," this man received an additional blessing from Jesus. Some scholars believe that all ten lepers received freedom from the disease, but only the one who returned to say "thank You" received complete physical restoration.

"Thank you." Two simple words that acknowledge your appreciation to the giver. The Bible tells us that every good and perfect gift comes from God.

We owe our gratitude to God for every good thing we experience in life. Failing to say "thank You" holds back the fullness of God's blessing in your life. Look for ways to show your appreciation to God today.

PRAYER

*Father God, I love You. Thank You for all the good things
You've given me. In Jesus' name, amen.*

Reaching Teach

Remember now your Creator in the days of your youth,
before the difficult days come.

ECCLESIASTES 12:1

E dward Teach was a natural leader. He must have developed a knack for motivating men to do things they didn't want to do. After developing a keen knowledge of the ways of the sea, Teach would have been a tremendous asset to any Navy. He probably could have been a celebrated admiral.

Instead, Teach allowed a lust for money and things to dissuade him from such an honorable existence. In the early 1700's, Teach became a vicious pirate.

Traveling from England, he took a ship called *Queen Anne's Revenge* and began to terrorize the waters of the Atlantic. Soon the coasts of Virginia and the Carolinas fell victim to his raids.

In Charleston, South Carolina, 1717, Teach used *Queen Anne's Revenge* to block the harbor, capturing any ship that tried to enter. He and his crew held citizens at ransom, only leaving after being given a large chest of medicine.

Soon Teach and his crew were so feared that it had a tremendous impact on shipping all along the American coast. Finally, farmers rallied together in an effort to capture Teach and his men.

Battling bitterly to the end, Teach fought hard with his sword and gun, only to fall dead with some 25 wounds to his body. After having pursued happiness in all the wrong places, Edward Teach, the man we know as "Blackbeard," died a miserable death. His death was not mourned, but celebrated.

The tragedy of Edward Teach was not just that he was of low moral character. The real tragedy was that he was a tremendous leader and a gifted sailor with unlimited potential for good,

LIVE ON PURPOSE TODAY

Set extra time in your day just to remember your Creator. Think about Him every day.

but no one was able to reach him. No one was able to
show him how to connect with his Creator in the days of
his youth.

One of the most important things you can do as a
young person is to get to know God for yourself. Leaning
on the beliefs of your family just doesn't cut it.

If you are going to reach your full potential as a
human being, it is imperative that you know God. To know
God, you must spend time with Him and study His Word.

PRAYER

*Father God, thank You for those who've shown me
how to connect with You. Help me to know You more
intimately every day. In Jesus' name, amen.*

Draw Near

Come near to God, and God will come near to you.
You sinners, clean sin out of your lives. You who are
trying to follow God and the world at the
same time, make your thinking pure.

JAMES 4:8 NCV

I remember when I wasn't that close to God. I wasn't as happy as I am now. I just wanted to hang out with my older friends at church instead of going to the class that was specifically for my age. I thought I wanted to be more like these friends, but even though I was hanging around with them, I still wasn't happy. I always had a feeling that I needed to go to that class. I guess that was the Holy Spirit drawing me in. One day I did go. When I went there the first time, the pastor quoted a Scripture I have never forgotten. It answered why God wasn't close to me before. The Scripture is James 4:8. It says that when you draw close to God, He will draw close to you. God was waiting on me. All that time I was thinking the wrong thing. Now if I start feeling a long way from God, I just draw near. I talk to God and read my Bible. Then God draws near to me. It's great.

LIVE ON PURPOSE

People will never satisfy your soul; only God can. God is waiting on you. He will never violate your free will. If you want to be closer to God, just draw near. Draw near today.

PRAYER

Lord, I want to be closer to You. Help me not to be distracted by the things of this world so that it steals my time with You. Help me to keep the right priorities in my life, in Jesus' name.

Only the Strong Forgive

{ *Even as Christ forgave you, so you also must do.* }

HEBREWS 6:12

Pride. That sting you feel when someone has wronged you. It plays to your sense of justice and righteousness. It cries out to your flesh, "Stand up for yourself!"

But pride is the number one enemy to forgiveness. Pride tells us that to forgive means to give up. The common misconception is that forgiveness is a form of weakness and failure.

Not one person who has ever lived had more wrongs to forgive than Jesus Christ. People mocked Him, lied about Him, publicly tried to humiliate Him, and even attempted to kill Him. His own friends denied knowing Him and betrayed Him.

There were people that Christ loved who hated Him. They belittled Him and questioned the motives behind the good things He did. They called Him names and physically beat Him.

In the hours when Christ could have most used the comfort and support of people, no human decency could be found. Christ was brutally beaten, stripped of His clothes, spat upon, and murdered.

Pride must have tried to sting Him deeply. "See if Elijah will come save Him," cried one of those who had gathered at the cross. "If You are the Christ, save Yourself and us!" blasphemed one of the thieves crucified next to Him. These statements and others were motivated by Satan to appeal to fleshly pride.

LIVE ON PURPOSE TODAY

Search your heart today. Is there any unforgiveness? If so, forgive that person right away!

In the face of the most brutal hatred the world has ever seen, Christ Jesus, our Lord, had the strength to push away from pride and to say, "Father, forgive them, for they do not know what they do."

That's real strength. *That's* real power. Christ displayed to the world what kind of strength it takes to forgive. The Roman centurion saw the strength of Christ and said, "Truly this Man was the Son of God."

Pride will try to work its way into every scenario in which you are hurt, leading you to hold grudges against people. Unforgiveness has more of an effect on you than it does on those who've wronged you.

If you are a Christian, you have been given the power of God through Christ to forgive. Make a decision today to stand against pride and be strong enough to forgive.

PRAYER

Lord Jesus, enable me to forgive those who
have wronged me. In Jesus' name, amen.

Explosive New Year

For He shall give His angels charge over you....

PSALM 91:11

The Bostwicks' New Year's Eve bash was always exciting. Our custom was to meet at the Bostwicks' home and hang out for a while. Later, we'd make our way to their farmhouse.

There we would drink hot apple cider, burn a huge bonfire fueled by recently discarded Christmas trees, and light off fireworks. My friend Price and I usually spent the entire time shooting bottle rockets.

The best part of the farmhouse, however, was the trip out there and back. Our coed group of 25 or so teenagers and 20-somethings usually bundled up together for a hayride or something.

One year, our transport vehicle was an open-air trolley-type trailer, like you might see at an amusement park. After spending a couple of hours at the farmhouse, it was time to head back to the Bostwicks' home.

I happened to be one of the first few people back on the trailer. Since it was so cold, I knew most of the girls were going to bundle up in the large floor area. That's where I headed. While I was getting situated on the floor at one end, my friend Helton boarded at the other.

At that exact moment, Price had just lit his last bottle rocket. Somehow, he thought it would be funny to freak Helton out by throwing the bottle rocket into the floor of the trailer. He hadn't seen those of us down in the floor!

I heard the hiss of the bottle rocket coming my way. Reflexively, I leaned back to dodge it. Leaning back, however, opened up the back of my sweater.

LIVE ON PURPOSE TODAY

Begin to memorize the full chapter of Psalm 91 today!

Fluke of flukes, the bottle rocket (still lit) landed inside my sweater. I fell on my back and BOOM! The bottle rocket exploded against my bare flesh. "Aaahhh!" I shouted. I was stunned!

A handful of people saw the whole thing. From their perspective, however, it looked like I was a hero! They thought I saw the bottle rocket coming and deliberately jumped on it. This was definitely not the case.

I do believe real heroes were on the scene though. As I reached back, I felt the area of skin that was burned, but somehow there wasn't a lot of pain. That errant bottle rocket could have done exponentially more damage than it did that night. God's angels protected my friends and me from the worst.

Christians have a covenant with God that provides protection. God gives His angels charge over us to ensure it. When faced with immediate danger, we can remind God of His promise and rest assured that He will keep it.

PRAYER

Father in heaven, thank You for Your promise to protect me and my family. In Jesus' name, amen.

Acknowledgments

Harrison House would like to thank the following people for the stories they contributed to this work:

Stephen Posey

Joshua Childs

Alyssa Whisner

Amy Sarker

Trecie Williams

Sarah Wehrli

Amanda Moringo

Prayer of Salvation

God loves you—no matter who you are, no matter what your past. God loves you so much that He gave His one and only begotten Son for you. The Bible tells us that "...whoever believes in him shall not perish but have eternal life" (John 3:16). Jesus laid down His life and rose again so that we could spend eternity with Him in heaven and experience His absolute best on earth. If you would like to receive Jesus into your life, say the following prayer out loud and mean it from your heart.

Heavenly Father, I come to You admitting that I am a sinner. Right now, I choose to turn away from sin, and I ask You to cleanse me of all unrighteousness. I believe that Your Son, Jesus, died on the cross to take away my sins. I also believe that He rose again from the dead so that I might be forgiven of my sins and made righteous through faith in Him. I call upon the name of Jesus Christ to be the Savior and Lord of my life. Jesus, I choose to follow You and ask that You fill me with the power of the Holy Spirit. I declare that right now I am a child of God. I am free from sin and full of the righteousness of God. I am saved in Jesus' name. Amen.

If you prayed this prayer to receive Jesus Christ as your Savior for the first time, please contact us on the Web at **www.harrisonhouse.com** to receive a free book.

Or you may write to us at

Harrison House
P.O. Box 35035
Tulsa, Oklahoma 74153

Live the Life You
Were Born To Live

Destiny is built on thousands of moments—opportunities to seek God's will, to seek His direction in the experience of every day. Let the *Life on Purpose Series* encourage you to make the most of every moment.

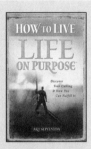

How To Live Your Life on Purpose™
ISBN 1-57794-321-X

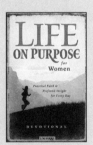

Life on Purpose™ *for Women*
ISBN 1-57794-649-9

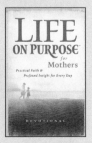

Life on Purpose™ *for Mothers*
ISBN 1-57794-683-9

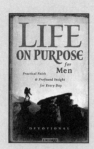

Life on Purpose™ for Men
ISBN 1-57794-648-0

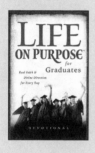

Life on Purpose™ for Graduates
ISBN 1-57794-727-4

Available at fine bookstores everywhere or visit
www.harrisonhouse.com.

DO THE EVOLUTION.

No, not the monkey thing. Evolution is change—steady, consistent, everyday change. Are you ready for a Oneighty® in your life? Then take the challenge. Give God five minutes of your day and watch the change begin.

The Oneighty® Devotional is as simple as 1-8-0. Study "1" Scripture a day. Commit to "8" weeks. Take the "0" pledge.

When you complete the *Oneighty® Devotional,* the Word of God will be more real and alive to you than ever before. Your mind will be renewed, and you will experience a 180-degree turn that will change your relationships, your prayer life, your self-esteem, and every other area of your life.

Oneighty® Devotional
by Blaine Bartel
1-57794-519-0

Available at bookstores everywhere or visit www.harrisonhouse.com.

when it's time to move on

1. find your life's quest

2. find your place to belong

3. find friends for life

4. bartel—the Oneighty guy. over twenty years of congratulating graduates. over twenty years of counseling graduates. now you can find the answers.

Little Black Book for Graduates
1-57794-612-X

THE FUTURE IS YOURS.

Load Up Pocket Devotional
1-57794-651-0

What you do with your life determines the future. You are only one person, but God can take one person and change nations. In the prophetic age that we live, He is looking for nation changers. That may sound unreal, but with God it is absolutely possible. These 31 devotions can revolutionize your future. Get to know God and take hold of your future.

PRAY WITH POWER

Prayers That Avail Much for Graduates
1-57794-664-8

With school behind you and a mountain of decision and responsibilities ahead of you, you need the strength of God's Word to see you through. *Prayers That Avail Much® for Graduates* makes it easier than ever to tap into God's wisdom through prayers based on His Word. You can pray with confidence knowing you are praying what God has already promised for you in His Word.

Prayers include:

- God's Wisdom and His Will

- Finances

- Finding Favor With Others

- Equipped for Success

- Your Future Spouse

- To Live Free From Worry

- When You Feel Lonely

- And More!

Available at bookstores everywhere
or visit www.harrisonhouse.com.

www.harrisonhouse.com

Fast. Easy. Convenient!

- ◆ New Book Information
- ◆ Look Inside the Book
- ◆ Press Releases
- ◆ Bestsellers

- ◆ Free E-News
- ◆ Author Biographies
- ◆ Upcoming Books
- ◆ Share Your Testimony

For the latest in book news and author information, please visit us on the Web at www.harrisonhouse.com. Get up-to-date pictures and details on all our powerful and life-changing products. Sign up for our e-mail newsletter, *Friends of the House,* and receive free monthly information on our authors and products including testimonials, author announcements, and more!

Harrison House—
Books That Bring Hope, Books That Bring Change

The Harrison House Vision

Proclaiming the truth and the power

Of the Gospel of Jesus Christ

With excellence;

Challenging Christians to

Live victoriously,

Grow spiritually,

Know God intimately.